entrance to the Sino-Soviet Friendship Building in Shanghai; Sun Yat-sen's desk; the assembly line in a Nanking truck factory.

LOVE AND HATE IN CHINA

books by Hans Koningsberger:

THE GOLDEN KEYS

THE AFFAIR

AN AMERICAN ROMANCE

A WALK WITH LOVE AND DEATH

I KNOW WHAT I'M DOING

LOVE AND

HATE IN CHINA

HANS KONINGSBERGER

McGRAW-HILL BOOK COMPANY
NEW YORK TORONTO LONDON

Printed in the United States of America.

Library of Congress Catalog Card Number: 66-19286
First Edition
35321

A portion of the contents of this book, in somewhat different form, appeared originally in *The New Yorker*.

Lu Hsun's short story "Kung I-Chi" was translated by Yang Hsien-yi and Gladys Yang for the Foreign Languages Press in Peking.

Cover and endpaper photographs by Hans Koningsberger.

Cover photograph: A poster on the wall of the Chi Wang Lou (Chamber of Beautiful Expectation) in a Peking park, which announces "an art exhibit in support of the people of Vietnam against American aggression."

LOVE AND HATE IN CHINA

1

THE SUMMERS OF PEKING are as vile as those in New York; and in Peking too, people tell each other, "It's not the heat, It's the humidity." Indeed, both cities lie at the eastern edge of a continent and both are at about forty degrees northern latitude. Those forty-latitude city summers are so very much worse than the real tropics, of course, because the houses and life in general cannot be adapted to the heat: in Peking as in New York the winters are grey, cold, icy and sleety. But both towns have a marvelous Indian summer with a limitless blue sky and nostalgic, heartbreaking sunsets.

And that is about where the similarities end. No two places could be farther apart in all senses of those words; and no two societies right now seem more different than China and the United States. Those differences, though, are themselves somewhat different from what people, here and over there, are told. The American public's idea of China is at least as wrong as the Chinese image of America. This is rather terrifying, but it seems dictated by the present course of history, comparable perhaps to the abyss between Catholics and Protestants in the sixteenth century which not even Erasmus could bridge. (Only many years and many million dead later was the edge taken off that confrontation and, it may seem, not because people had become wiser or more tolerant or better informed about the other side, but because they did not care too much any more.)

Peking is in its seventeenth year as capital of a communistic China and, say, in its one thousand and first year as capital of Imperial China—both called, and both considered, by their inhabitants *Zung Ghuo,* the Central Country, or Middle Kingdom as it used to be translated into English.

"China" is written 中国; the first sign clearly indicating "middle," and the second one "country": it is a stylization of an armed man in a field. At a diplomatic reception in Peking, a French student said, "Maybe the Chinese think that Peking is the center of the world; but we're no different; the French believe that Paris is the center of the world." "But Paris is the center of the world," the Agence France Presse correspondent in Peking answered him coldly.

Do not visualize Peking as a new Metropolis, a sinister Orwellian capital of seven hundred million souls, nor as an oriental Moscow filled with gingerbread government offices in the style Stalin admired, nor as an enlarged American Chinatown with political slogans instead of advertisements and thin waistlines instead of bulging ones. Some of Peking, its poorest streets, are like Djakarta on Java, at least during the hot months; apart from that, it isn't reminiscent of any other capital. Peking rarely gives the feeling of a big city, although it has seven million people within its boundaries. The wide avenues, the new buildings, and the old gates, temples, and palaces are but a very loose grid, stuffed as it were with dozens of villages. These are Asian villages in that their inhabitants pursue a good deal of their activities in the street or in sight of the street; they dine, have their hair cut, wash their babies, buy and sell, on the sidewalks. They are very un-Asian in being clean, without smells, without beggars, and even without flies.

The daily comings and goings of the people look terribly normal. They seem neither "blue ants" (as a widely quoted journalist called them) slaving away, nor eager revolutionaries, chin upward marching into glory. They surely do not work as hard as the American experts fear and their own government may hope: any number of them can be observed sitting on benches nursing cigarets and staring into space. Tien Chiao, the fairground at the southern city gate, is still in full swing, and its shows, cabarets, and operas on any afternoon are filled to the last seat with men who seem to have as little to do or to worry about as a Yonkers Raceway crowd. In one show, a magician pulls a red flag out of a hat which bears the words, "Strength through Self-reliance," but the audience takes that in its stride and goes on complacently picking its teeth. Road-mending crews have that same air of defiant, trade-unionistic slowness which New York City workers have brought to such a peak of perfection.

Men and women, four years after the catastrophes of the Great Leap and the great drought, seem quieter, but also less grim and more content than the Chinese of Singapore or the Indians of Calcutta. They look well fed and reasonably dressed. There is quite a lot of color in their appearance, and every now and again someone stands out who is actually elegant by any standards—a girl, for instance, in a Pucci-type dress, on high heels, with marvelously coiffed hair, a black parasol, and even with that distant, slightly haughty look which beautiful women all over the world sport in public. The people of Peking look better off than they were in the chaotic years before 1949, but apart from that they continue to look like just-people through all the overwhelming changes in public philosophy, morale, and their very raison d'être—a human quality of stubbornness which through the ages has enraged and frustrated reformers and revolutionaries while comforting others.

Peking, though, is very much in flux. Centuries seem to march through it as once did the camel caravans from Mongolia. The Forbidden City, being restored, looks again more or less as Marco Polo found it in Khan-Balik, but schoolchildren with red Pioneer scarves now play hopscotch where Kublai Khan used to play with his Thousand Women. Old men still sing in falsetto voices and do calisthenics at dawn on Coal Hill. Factories belch smoke. Cadres deliver Brave New World lectures to deputees from Sinkiang and Tibet. In an alleyway, an old, old woman in a sarong, her shriveled breasts bare, cooks her supper of rice and vegetables in an iron pot on a charcoal fire. Little boys have card games at tables in front of their houses, or in the evening under a street light right in the mildle of the road; men play checkers in the shadow of the old gate towers. The famous city walls are being torn down and have almost gone. A silversmith pains-takingly boards up his shop window with numbered planks. Swallows circle through the sky in patterns as if posing for a bamboo paper print. Cicadas sing in the trees and crickets in little reed cages hanging against doorposts. Neon advertise-ments blink from rooftops. Hungarian- and Chinese-made buses dash through the streets.

And, riding in one of these, just after nightfall, with a threat of rain in the air, standing hemmed in by people going home and too preoccupied to stare much, the lights of shops and lampposts streaking by, and a conductress with a tired smile counting out your change, you may of a sudden feel that Peking is soon going to be a big city like any other, that its strangenesses should be enjoyed while they last, because one day it will be as sophisticated, incoherent, slick and hard as New York.

2

WALLS, TYPICALLY, used to be the most striking feature of Peking. The town has the contour of two boxes lying against each other, like this: ⊥.

The square box was called the Tartar Town and the oblong one the Chinese Town. Within the square box was another walled box, the Imperial City, and within that still another one, the Forbidden City. All those walls had the very real function of preventing the populace from going where they pleased; through the centuries, China has been at war with itself. After the Manchus had captured Peking in 1644 and established their dynasty, the Tartar Town became the exclusive residence for them and their Chinese collaborators. But even when the last emperor had been overthrown in 1911, the Forbidden City remained forbidden; and by that time the Western nations had added another out-of-bounds spot, Legation Quarter, which almost stopped up the gap left between the southern wall of the Imperial City and the northern wall of the Chinese Town. Part of that wall looked down upon Legation Quarter, and here Western troops patrolled and Western ladies and gentlemen strolled evenings and Sundays after church. Unlike Shanghai Park, the promenade was open to dogs, but like that park, closed to Chinamen.

Until 1949, the gates in the outer city wall were closed at eight in the evening in summer, and in winter at twilight; Peking was the last big town in the world to fit its days in such a medieval frame. It had reason to do so, for life was as insecure as in the worst time of the empire. By then Peking (the name means "Northern Capital") had been rechristened by Chiang Kai-shek into Peiping which is "Northern Peace," and the capital had been moved to Nanking. In 1949, when the Communist government took the town, they made it the capital once more and gave it back its name Peking. The U.S. State Department (off and on) and most American mapmakers go on talking about the nonexistent town of Peiping and putting it in atlases; an interesting example of a nominalistic, well-nigh old-Chinese view of reality. It is reminiscent of that Ming emperor who, instead of bothering with dike building, changed the name of a wild river from "The Wild One" to "The Peaceful One." It didn't help.

The beautiful gate towers of Peking have been left standing, with their double and triple roofs curving upward at the points—exactly as once the tents of the Golden Horde did. A few stretches of wall are left, too; the city has spread beyond them in housing developments, factories, schools, and student dormitories. Chinese archaeologists regret it; one predicted that in one or two generations everyone will mourn those vanished walls, including party officials who, in his words, "could not in time overcome their prejudices." But the same has happened from Paris to Samarkand; it is not difficult to see how the tearing down of medieval walls ("feudal walls," they would say in China) must provide post-revolution city planners with an almost sensual pleasure. The Forbidden City is now the Palace Museum, and Legation Quarter, probably the sorest spot of all to local sensitivities, is just some city blocks like any others. Its main street is still called "Legation Street" by the few Westerners in Peking, and a letter with that address will reach its destination. It is pretty and shady, and it again houses a number of diplomatic posts: the Rumanians, the Indians, the Burmese, and the East Germans (the last one in an ornate building behind red lacquered columns; the Germans are as busy as beavers in China). The only original Western mission left in the street is that of the Dutch, who have a cluster of charming houses, in old Dutch East Indies fashion, around a lawn with shade trees and even a swimming pool, the one diplomatic pool in town and thus a social center of gravity. (A nonswimming visitor to the mission is an old Chinese lady who was once lady-in-waiting to the last empress and who dresses, looks, and talks as if nothing whatsoever has changed; she speaks impeccable socialite British, and her one, but bitter, complaint seemed to be about an English writer who had misspelled her name in a recent book.) The Dutch are on notice to pack up, as though the Chinese government feels nervous as long as any of the masters from the old days remains in his traditional spot. They may have to move

—like the English and the French before them—to one of the new buildings put up for foreigners far from the center of town, air-conditioned, shadeless horrors in New Jersey neo-suburban style. The one-time American embassy, next to the Dutch, is now used as a guest house for foreign V.I.P.'s—it usually stands empty, with a lonely gardener squatting amidst the well-kept lawns, smoking or feeding his chickens. The International Club is still the International Club, with a swimming pool too. Under the new Chinese law everyone who uses the pool for the first time must produce a doctor's certificate that he has no contagious disease. The club's members, mainly Westerners, think such fanatical cleanliness almost as strangely oriental as their fathers did the traditional Chinese dirtiness. The club has a "dependance" two hours to the northwest of the town, beyond the Chuyungkuan Pass, the old invasion route to the capital. It is a lovely restaurant in the hills, with a terrace surrounded with flowers and with nothing less than the Great Wall for a backdrop. It is probably the only public place in the country where Chinese visitors are not admitted; you'd almost expect to see a Diners Club sign on the wall.

Peking has very good restaurants, run on a joint state-private basis which accounts for their individuality; the best one is called "The Garden of Pleasure" and it lives up to the name by the elaborateness and leisure of its service. One reserves a table here (by telephone: China is again such terra incognita that it seems useful to fill in these trivial details); guests are received in an anteroom with little cups of tea and liqueur, hot towels, and a discussion of the menu and its time table with the headwaiter. This may sound unbelievable or at least incongruous in "the capital of revolutionary communism," but that is how it is. The last edition of the Peking Guidebook (1960) lists thirty-five good restaurants, not including those in the hotels. They are not patronized by some new master class, but by the general public. Couples sit here, drinking tea and smoking cigarets, and groups of girl students acting very self-possessed and modern. They look at the men, and the men look at them. It is not the Champs Elysées, but neither is it the a-romantic, sexless desert which so many Western writers have reported.

And outside, in the evening darkness under the trees, couples sit holding hands, or the girl leans with her head against the boy's shoulder, or they may even be mildly necking—a more revisionistic spectacle than one would expect to find anywhere east of Moscow.

3

IN THE SIMPLE SYMMETRY of Peking's avenues, Tien An Men Square forms the focal point. Here indeed is monumentality suiting a capital. *Men* means gate, and Tien An Men is the Gate of Heavenly Peace. It closes off the north side of the square named after it, and makes the background to all those photographs of May Day parades and October 1 celebrations; it has the hierarchical and hieratic role filled by Lenin's tomb against the Kremlin wall in Moscow, and here one may expect that Mao Tse-tung will be buried one day. Tien An Men dates back to the Ming emperors of the late Middle Ages and its red brick walls have a marvelous patina; on each side, somewhat jarring wooden boards with inscriptions read: "Long Live the Chinese People's Republic!" and "Long Live the Unity of the Peoples of the World!" (The

Western exclamation mark has been incorporated in the list of Chinese characters.) Tours of the Imperial City begin at Tien An Men, and in front of it tourists, soldiers on leave, and classes of schoolchildren pose to have their pictures taken by each other or by the photographer of the square who lugs one of those old machines on a tripod, with a black cloth to tuck his head under.

The east and west side of the square are taken up by two new buildings, the Museum of Chinese History, and the Great Hall of the People—both, as visitors are told repeatedly, put up in only ten months. They look alike, and have long, low façades with columns and pseudo-pillars in light stone—the kind of architecture American congressmen like too. Looking south, Tien An Men faces the great axial road through Chien Men, once the gate of the Tartar Town. There is a little park here with benches which serves on summer evenings as a lover's lane. Chien Men is one of the classical Peking beauty spots and as such has to be savored at a specific time: when the full moon stands directly above the gate. The Marco Polo Bridge, to name another one, must be seen under a waning moon, and the imperial stone informing the traveler so still stands. Topping the axial road through Chien Men is Changan Avenue, a boulevard which has eight or ten car lanes and seems even wider than it is because of an absence of cars to fill all those lanes. There is very little motor traffic in Chinese towns; the vastness of Tien An Men Square and its boulevards is softened only by clusters of pedestrians almost lost within that stone desert. Its unrelieved emptiness actually makes it one of the depressing sights in Peking, which of course does not stop proud officials from bringing visitors here rather than to the bustle of other districts. Only on a summer's night does the square achieve a new mood, when hundreds of families come to it for their fresh air, and, sitting or lying in Chinese fashion on straw mats wherever they want to, mitigate the harshness of the lack of human scale in this project. Changan Avenue (the name means "Perpetual Peace") has a street-light system of Parisian brightness; the difference is that to save electricity it is used only at certain hours and on certain occasions—for instance when a foreign statesman is guest at a banquet in the Great Hall of the People. It is soothing to walk in the square once all those big lights have been extinguished; there is a vague glimmer left then of lamps here and there, and maybe of the moon, points of light from cigarets, soft voices of people, and, rarely, the sound of a truck. Peking becomes very still at night.

Tien An Men was the gate through which the emperor left the Imperial City for the yearly sacrifices to Heaven and Earth which alone preserved the harmony of man and nature, and from here all his edicts were issued. A visitor needs to wrap himself in such historical and literary reminiscences to be properly impressed by the Imperial City which has in common with some other famous sights of the world that by itself —if one dares admit it—it is rather disappointing. It must have presented an overwhelming spectacle in the days when it was filled with the thousands of officials, servants, concubines, and soldiers of the Imperial household. Now, empty but for the Eternal Tourists—here, too, with cameras—it does not come to life any more, and its ever-repeated architectural pattern becomes, sacrilegious as it may sound, just boring.

Temples and palaces as remembrances from a dead past, the monumental thoroughfares and the teeming narrow side-streets, the throngs of pedestrians in all kinds of getups and speaking a dozen dialects (many newly in from the countryside), the scarcity of wheeled traffic, all give Peking a touch of Europe—of an Italian town, perhaps, in the sixteenth century. Fitting within that era is the role foreigners play: there are many emissaries from faraway countries, but little contact, no mass travel across the frontiers. Especially in this respect, Peking must look once more as it did three hundred years ago. It should be remembered that Marco Polo, traveling with relative ease, happened to arrive here during a short foreign occupation of China by the Mongols who needed foreign collaborators to keep the Chinese in their places. The next prominent visitor to Peking, Matteo Ricci of the Society of Jesus in the year 1601, had needed nineteen years to work his way up here from Macao. (Ricci was perhaps the most civilized European ever to set foot in China and he has remained about the only one who ever became a member of Peking society. Those who followed behaved so atrociously that soon the Chinese reverted to their belief in segregation.)

Foreign ministers or heads of state now visiting Peking invariably receive the local equivalent of a ticker tape parade: a flags and flowers parade from the airport to the Great Hall of the People. In China's total isolation from the power centers of the world, every one of them, no matter how tiny his country, is important and demonstrates to the people that China is not forgotten and unloved. There must be a complicated schedule in operation indicating which school classes get off when, in order to set out and line Changan Avenue at the right hour and place. The children participating in these welcomes look happy, as children do everywhere when skipping class, and the colorfulness of their dresses or blouses, the flags, balloons, and huge bouquets of artificial flowers they carry, add up to a festiveness bound to impress a visitor, no matter how unspontaneous it all may be. These vast crowds of cheering children are one of Peking's main assets in introducing itself.

But once the distinguished foreign visitor is in town, his environment undergoes a change for the worse, and some very determined dinners and sight-seeing with speeches follow. The banquets are attended by the entire diplomatic corps minus those countries which may be on nonspeaking terms with the visitor, by the press, including the complete Western press (three men), and by a selection of officials; they are the highlights on Peking's not very intense social calendar. However, while the diplomats may bring their wives, the officials and the journalists have to come alone; any Chinese lady in the hall is there under her own professional steam.

On these occasions the food is marvelous, the conversation flagging. Engraved in my mind is the visit of the President of Somalia, a man who probably speaks impeccable Italian but who for clear political reasons had to use another language. He chose English. He stumbled over many words and, unfortunately, did not skip these—everyone held a copy of his text anyway, and a Chinese translation followed—but repeated his slips until he felt he had them right. The word "people" bothered him especially; every time he started it in two syllables, pee-o. ("People" and "peoples" are words that occur frequently in this type of speech). His address, in which he appealed several times to the United Nations, would have left his Chinese audience rather cold anyway; it was generally endured in agonized silence. At my table, which consisted of a journalist from the People's Republic of Mongolia, one from

Bulgaria, one from Pakistan, one from East Germany, myself, and two people from the Ministry of Foreign Affairs, nothing was said for a long time afterward. Finally, as we were wrestling to get some very slippery shrimp between our chopsticks, the Foreign Ministry lady beside me bent over and said to me, "Are there many Chinese restaurants in Warsaw?" It was by all standards a surprising gambit, for she could not possibly have thought I was a Pole. When I had managed to answer that I did not know, the band had struck up one of those lively airs which blissfully drown all talk, and thus I never found out if and how she was going to connect this surrealistic question with Somalia, me, or the shrimp.

4

THE HISTORY OF CHINA has been de-chaoticized. All those centuries of bloodshed, plunder and misery have been straightened, miraculously and Marxistically, into one clear, upward path. Thus, the central Museum of Chinese History on the east side of Tien An Men Square presents it, and thus a hundred million children in the new grade schools are taught. This is no small matter. The West had its brief spell of a similar euphoria, around the year 1890 or so, when it seemed (to the well-fed, well-dressed, well-washed, anyway) that history made eminent sense and that all its events had finally led up to a scientific, rational earth, benevolently run by the white race. It was a nice idea, no doubt still nostalgically clung to by quite a number of people, and any Victorian autobiography can demonstrate how much strength and happiness it gave its believers. The new Chinese view is a similar source of strength, but more so, for it is universal and official dogma. Chinese history is now neatly divided into a Primitive Society ending around four thousand years ago, a Slave Society from 2000 B.C. until 475 B.C., a Feudal Society lasting until the Opium War of 1840, and then the semi-colonial and revolutionary era leading to the Liberation of 1949. It is quite simple to see the great events of those forty centuries as outcomes of class war, and to discuss their products, from siege machines to porcelain drinking cups, as mirroring class societies. And the area of Chinese historical experience is so huge and has been so isolated, that it makes for a marvelous social laboratory for determinism: one can predict nicely that so much oppression over such and such a time will lead to one more peasant rebellion, one more period of civil war, one more new dynasty.

All this is Chinese rather than Marxist perhaps, but China has never had Russia's trouble of fitting patriotism in with Marxism, for China has mostly been "on the right side" from a Communist point of view: either suffering in the vast majority of its population under some often foreign, despot, or government and people both being underdogs to the whole world. Thus the great art from China's past is exhibited in the museum as demonstrating at the same time the superior skill of the simple craftsman and the irresponsible luxuries of the idle rich (as it does, of course); and the terrible wars and the humiliations of the past hundred years demonstrate the courage of the peasants, the cruelty of the ruling classes (East or West), and the unavoidable *sense* of the Revolution. The violence and horrors which made life a senseless blank to the peasants and a nightmare to the intellectuals, now are shown to have had their reasons; history has been provided with a happy ending. At the exit of the museum, in a text written by Mao Tse-tung in red letters on gold, it says so. And China was the chosen setting.

In this philosophy, even the break with Russia is a good thing. Russia was the only peacetime ally China ever had, and one cannot help but feel that the Chinese are actually relieved it is over. They may have lost some years and a lot of blueprints and experts, but the feeling that they are really going it alone again, as always, needing no one, more than makes up for that. Communism, purified and improved, has been nationalized in the process; its origin as an "alien creed" helped it as little in Peking as in Dallas.

What supports the Chinese visitor to the museum in this solipsist view of history is that the Chinese, unlike the Russians, *indeed* invented almost everything: paper, silk, porcelain, gunpowder, cannon, the compass, printing, paper money. In 1793 the Chinese emperor had his famous message delivered to the British emissary: "We do not have the slightest need of your country's manufactures"; in 1966 the director of the Nanking automobile works said of his truck: "All auto workers learn from other countries, but this is all our own design." Can anyone in the West fathom how proud these people are, and how this pride was bound to explode after having been squeezed in a vise for so long? Or, for that matter, can anyone in the West fathom how hated foreigners really were, all of us, the sweet missionary and the understanding Pearl Buck-type writer, and how hated we still are —and not the least by those Chinese who need us (always an unforgivable relationship), from the Hong Kong Hilton busboys to Chiang Kai-shek?

The crucial battles of Chinese history are shown in modern paintings by the museum, with the same abundant detail and total absence of artistry one can find in historical reconstructions of *Life* magazine. But interesting is that, amidst the gore, the heroes of these scenes are all drawn with more or less Caucasian features. Why on earth? There are several explanations; a gentle one has it that thus the official view of history tones down the element of "race" in warfare. It seems more plausible—bad as it would be both for Chinese pride and for Western smugness—that a Caucasian (that is, European) type of beauty or manliness appeals most to modern Chinese aesthetics. This tallies with the political posters in which the young Chinese soldier or worker is usually drawn the way we would show a Frenchman or Italian, with just a touch of easternness around the eyes, and it tallies with the stars of the stage and the movies who all have a very Western type of beauty and who, on the stage, are moreover made up in Western color schemes, pale, with red cheeks. The Chinese do not call Westerners "white men" (we aren't, of course). Their slang designation, if not "foreign devils," is "the hairy ones" or "the big noses." When in a cabaret scene a Chinese actor has to personify an American soldier, he simply pastes on a big paper nose. Chinese on posters have pink complexions (there is actually a wide variety of racial types in China, from European pale to very dark); Westerners look a sickly yellow—if they are Americans, that is. The people from the Dominican Republic, who featured widely on the political posters of 1965, had nice tans (and beards).

5

THE FOREIGNER IN CHINA now stands out to such a degree that he disturbs whatever he observes. Also, he may find that his well-meaning neutrality (which most present-day visitors come with) crumbles under the endless frustrations of dealing with a Kafka-esque officialdom. It needs will power, some humor, and also luck, not to extrapolate from these strictly private and for-foreigners-only experiences to a general view, and not to soothe one's annoyances by a getting even in writing later. Isn't the popularity, for instance, of such countries as West Germany, Switzerland, and Spain with American visitors at least partly based on the obsequiousness of their officials and hotel keepers toward the prosperous foreigner? In China it is now, in many matters, the other way around: foreigners are not treated better but worse than natives. (A Chinese can travel freely, a foreigner needs a travel permit for each town.) After so many years in which the reverse was true, it seems unfair to protest this too much. It isn't that difficult, either, to get away from the official side of life; "You will love this town when you're walking in it, alone," a Western diplomat in Peking tells his guests, and most foreigners share that feeling at most times.

Officials, guides, and interpreters are forever selling their country and its system to visitors, and, predictably, from our point of view they go about it the wrong way; exaggerating facts, they sow unjustified doubts; insisting that everything is fine, they obscure those things which are; and being—like every Asian east of the Israeli border—totally unable to poke fun at themselves, they seem intolerably smug. But all this is only the wrapping of China.

There was for instance the head of a "tea brigade" in the mountains near Hangchow, a section of a tea-growing commune. Here was a young man obnoxious in his self-righteousness, his lecturing attitude, and his dogmatism—precisely the "cadre worker" as we would picture him at his worst. But then this man took his guests around, and showed them the houses of the tea workers. He climbed a staircase with them, and pointed out the heavy wooden table this family had recently acquired, the two trunks, an alarm clock, and the large new oil lamp. (These tea peasants used to be so poor that all they had for light were burning pine tree roots.) He turned around, and as everyone started to climb down the stairs again, he gave the new tabletop one more caressing stroke. And suddenly the mood of this visit changed, suddenly this self-satisfied Communist seemed decent and also painfully pathetic in his pride over something we wouldn't give a thought. And the question arose, what right do we Westerners have, freshly back home from plundering the world for four centuries, fat and rich and worried about calories, what nerve do we have really, to poke around here and see if there's dust on the political piano, and worry so nobly whether these people, whose former drowning or starving by the millions didn't make our front pages, have enough democratic rights?

Being in China is full of such manic-depressive experiences for a foreigner: alternating boredom and annoyance with love and admiration. The foreign visitors who think everything is wonderful are probably not occupied with China but with their own dreams—unfortunately, for that way they convince very few people of anything. Then there are the travelers who note the material improvements they see, the housing, the food, and the hospitals, but who either ignore the spirit behind this or think it is a regrettable by-product which will vanish in time. China is taught a New Morality, and it is one by and for Communists, not Reform Democrats; it is as real as the housing and the hospitals and you cannot treat of one without the other. But if these men have learned in their mothers' laps that communism is Evil, they are faced with the problem: How can Evil produce good? They keep apologizing for their enthusiasm; in every other paragraph of their books you find a *Whether you like it or not, the Chinese now.* . . . This does not help them in the least to carry weight with the people of the far right who (a) will not read their books, and (b) are not worried about the Chinese being miserable, but powerful.

Remarkable are those who, without coming to China, write about horrors—as for instance J. Alsop who goes on unabashedly through the years predicting things which do not come true, and whose finest effort to date seems to me a piece about "Suppose Mao would order the murder of three hundred million Chinese and use their bodies for manure"—this in a country which has become almost as painstakingly careful about human lives as New Zealand. There are the China watchers in Washington and in the American Consulate General in Hong Kong, cubicles full of young men who read every line and in between every line to come out of China, and who probably know more about the grain harvest in Heilungkiang and the sugar shortage in Yunnan than anyone else inside or outside China, but whose very choice of words in talking about it shows that China is in essence the dark side of the moon to them—and who are living in a political climate that does not give them a fair chance to be otherwise. There are those feelings of ill will and superiority toward other races which have covered the Western world like fallout for so long that we all have got some of it in our bones. Although over the past fifty years the Western nations have been killing off each other's subjects to the tune of about one hundred million souls, we go on thinking of ourselves as having a special appreciation and respect for the (white) individual, and as having a special kind of civilizedness, not yet equaled elsewhere; a Chinese who spits or smacks succeeds quite easily in outweighing all our own crimes in our minds and proving the point.

Because of these pitfalls, I have tried to keep myself out of this book as much as possible. I am a citizen of Holland, which is why I could go at all, but the Chinese government kept me waiting more than four years for my visa, and they refused me most of my special requests once I was there; I arrived by way of Russia and left through Hong Kong.

I traveled alone and wandered around alone—of course, for there is no reason why the government would have a foreigner trailed; there is nothing he could see or do which would harm their country. They wouldn't give him permission to visit their atomic energy plants or some place in Sinkiang or Tibet where there was unrest; without a travel permit he cannot get on any train, and if there are indeed "underground Chinese" left working for Chiang Kai-shek, which no one in China believes, they wouldn't talk with a Westerner.

Interpreters are available, at a rate of eighty cents an hour, but a traveling writer or journalist who wants to manage without is free to do so. For each city or area, a permit is needed, a visa; when, for instance, I traveled from Nanking to Hangchow without at that time a visa for Shanghai where I had to change trains, I had to spend the hour in between in a foreigners' waiting room in the station, as if in transit on an airfield. (I shared the waiting room with a group of students from North Vietnam, who were treated precisely the same as I, a citizen of a NATO country, was. We were all equally outsiders.)

In some places I have been received marvelously, with all kinds of people coming up to shake hands and say something about the brotherhood of nations—and I have also been hemmed in and screamed at by a furious mob, for taking a picture of what they considered a slum street. Most of the repeatedly offered chances to interview officials I have avoided, even if by doing so I gave offense. The atmosphere in which those official briefings take place is heavy with unreality; you are under a spell, they become like a dream. The interviewer sits in a hot office, fans burring; one official reads off that the production of product X was 89% higher in 1965 than in 1960; another official stares into space and scratches his leg; a girl pours more tea. "Oh no, I mean 98% higher," the first official says, and dutifully the interviewer changes 89 to 98, and draws a cat or a cow in the margin of his notebook. And since these briefings might as well have taken place in Geneva or London instead of in China, they have to be interspersed with little items from the "When I got off the plane" and "The cabdriver told me" school of reporting, to provide some *couleur locale.* It takes oriental patience to participate in them, and probably also to read about them.

6

"CHINESE COOLIES LOVE TO EAT: as soon as they've made some money, they go spend it in a roadside eat house." This interesting sidelight on the food situation was thrown by two American writers in the year 1936 in their humorous guidebook to Shanghai. (Another sample of its wit: "When your rickshaw coolie starts to pant, you're approaching the Garden Bridge. . . .") In those gay thirties, twenty thousand dead coolies were collected each year from the sidewalks of Shanghai, where they had died of hunger, and carted off to potter's field.

Getting fed, the preoccupation of most men, women and children in this world, still plays a larger part in the daily life of China than of the West, but these days the food is there. City people buy their supplies from push carts, market stalls, and shops varying in size from a little booth with most of its stuff spread out on a mat on the sidewalk, to big stores with neon lights, plate-glass windows, and separate departments for meat products, sweets, cans, vegetables and fruits, beverages, and a collection of grains, rices, and beans. The big stores make nice displays, with mirrors behind them, flowers, *et al.*, with no atmosphere of scarcity and completely without that drabness which is found (except for some special stores in the capitals) in Communist Eastern Europe. And then, while in Russia they plunk your purchases on the counter, not letting you forget for a second that they're just state employees and don't really give a damn whether you buy or not, the service in China is overwhelming. The Chinese are unbelievably painstaking anyway, in whatever they do; store clerks are so polite and careful that they ruin a shopper for the Western world. A woman buys two cakes; the clerk invites her to make her choice out of a dozen which look totally alike; when she has decided, he wraps them up and ties a string around them as if it were a Christmas gift; while she counts out her pennies, he looks as if she made his day with her purchase. And everything is so very clean; in the departments where they sell bread and candies, the girls wear white mouth cloths (rather ghostlike); floors, it seems, are swept every ten minutes, and if a fly appears which has somehow survived the great Fly Purge of a few years ago, half the store sets out to catch it. (That purge concerned itself with what were called "the four pests," rats, flies, mosquitoes, and sparrows. A few sparrows have reappeared in the towns, and they are now left alone; the skies do not seem emptier than in our cities because of the swallows and after sunset the bats. The fly purge seems to have been almost total; even on a cattle-farm manure heap I didn't see one fly. It may have been expected that the gruesome war on the sparrows would have completely disturbed the ecology of the cities but for unexplained reasons this has not happened, and Peking has no more gnats or other insects than New York City.)

Though the shops look pretty, there are scarcities. Grain, which includes rice, and cotton are the two main rationed items—the Chinese officials do not talk about rationing but about "planned supply," which is not as deceptive as it may sound. When China had a free economy, most people, most of the time, had less than now through the very efficient rationing system of no-money; starving to death was then one of the most widely practiced free enterprises. It is difficult to get reliable ration figures for the present. The change since 1960–62, when rice, fats, tobacco, fish, meat, cotton, and sugar were in desperately short supply and restaurants were closed or forbiddingly expensive, is great; that much is certain. After the 1965 autumn harvest, the rice ration in the towns was one continental pound (1.1 lb.) per person per day, and very few people actually used that much. All other foods were unrationed and in good supply; the piles of fruit, vegetables and eggs made great slashes of color along the shopping streets. Towns are surrounded by market gardens which use their human manure; at peak harvest times they deluge their towns with produce. Last summer there were so many tomatoes in Peking that the price for the best quality went down to 20 fen (Chinese cents) for 10 kilos, which means 20 lbs. for 7 American cents. That was cheap even for the lowest-paid laborer. The availability of the other rationed item in the towns, cotton, is quoted as "two dresses a year," which gives an idea. Figures vary from place to place, and officials are loath to discuss this particular subject. Artificial fibers are unrationed, and the stores have good supplies of shirts and dresses in locally made material of the rayon and nylon type.

Factories and big offices run their own canteens. Here is a menu of an average canteen, in a machine factory: at the first window, they sold dumplings (4 for 6 fen), dry soya pancakes and Chinese bread (3 fen); at the second window, fried fish (15 fen), fried egg omelette (12 fen), potato with liver (14 fen), and enormous bowls of sticky rice for 5 fen. At the third window were two kinds of vegetables for 5 fen each; "three delicacies," a Canton dish, for 15 fen, chicken with soya beans for 18 fen, and pork in soya sauce, 15 fen. The helping of fish was small and bony, the chicken was good, the vegetables and the pork very nice. In the next chapter, an effort will be made to say something sensible about the real value of one fen, which is nominally four-tenths of an American penny.

In the countryside, things are more complex, fluctuating with local harvests, and involving premiums, of extra cotton for instance, for peasants who sell pork or eggs from their private plots to the state buying agency. The meat ration in the country is given as thirty pounds a year, but who can evaluate such a figure? Can every peasant anywhere indeed get his thirty pounds, and does he want them? Before the last war, in some areas peasants ate meat only once a year, during the New Year festival; and one can still visit communes where they say, "We're too poor to eat meat more than once a month or so."

In 1965, peasants were guaranteed 250 kilos of rice or wheat flour for themselves (a kilo is 2.2 lbs). That compares with the 135 kilos for light workers and 218 kilos for heavy workers in 1961 which Edgar Snow quotes. It would not seem a sensational improvement, but there are more side dishes now: fish, chicken, and vegetables are freely available. The most sensible way of summing it all up may be that, traveling through this vast country, looking for hours out of car or train windows, or walking along country lanes, one sees many poor people, many people working hard with the most primitive tools, but no one looking badly in need of more food. How such a person would look is unforgettable to anyone who has ever set foot in India—or in Haiti, or in the mountains of Mexico.

In 1961, dinner in a simple restaurant cost up to four American dollars; in 1962, the same dinner cost two dollars, and in 1965 the check was down to forty American cents. This strange deflation could occur only in a country where the government is free to set prices without direct relation to cost or profit; the price fall simply means that there is now enough food to have everyone in town eat in a real restaurant at times—everyone, that is, who is properly washed and has a clean shirt. (There is still a sub-proletarian class in the cities of ragged coolies hauling loads, presenting the gruesome spectacle, so well known before the war, of men working like draft animals. They have health and labor insurance now, but they are paid by the load only.)

"The Garden of Pleasure" in Peking now charges about two dollars for its most elaborate meal, which is top price for the town. A less expensive one is for instance a Mongolian restaurant in the northwest section, which has outdoor tables in summer and where a dinner for four cost 12 yuan or about five dollars. That included shaslik, mushrooms, stacks of side dishes, and elaborate egg-and-tomato soups, while everyone floated away on gallons of beer. (The soup is served last in China.) The native beer comes in big bottles and is good; then there is Maotai, a terrifying, brownish brandy in stone flasks, many wines, all home-grown, and something called and vaguely resembling whiskey. Only in two hotels in Peking are there bilingual menus and forks and spoons. Chinese food, which embraces endlessly more varieties than those presented in Chinese restaurants abroad, should of course be eaten with chopsticks, which comes quite easy if there is no alternative. With sticks, a guest can reach all the dishes on the table and pick from them at random, which is what he is supposed to do. It makes for more selective and for slower eating. With many foods, sticks are superior to forks and spoons, because with sticks the mouth touches only the food itself. With other dishes, such as crabs, sticks involve the eater in rather messy struggles.

In Hangchow, I ate fish caught in the lake the restaurant looked out on, a huge fish in a dark sweetish sauce tasting like Mexican *mole*. That dinner cost forty cents. But Canton, of course, is the center of it all—the only original school of *haute cuisine* to exist outside France. Canton has real specialty food shops; the fruit stores are a delight, having all we have plus mangoes, pomegranates, durians, litchis, and long-yan or dragon's eyes, tasting like a cross between plums and grapes; in Canton people still, or again, discuss their dinners like French gourmands. The Canton Pan Chi restaurant served a dinner of beef with leeks, followed by fish with krupuk (leaves of fried shrimp paste), bowls of green vegetables, rice, egg soup, and beer, for a dollar. One cannot do more than have a taste from each of these dishes, for Chinese menus—unlike Western ones—promise much less than the waiter actually brings. In my early days here, I thought the waiters would be appalled at the waste of food ordered and not eaten, but no one bats an eyelid. Perhaps it goes back into the pot. The Pan Chi is an elaborate place, with half a dozen rooms and terraces, some roofed and some open, grouped around little ponds and waterfalls in the old style, and it is packed every evening. The wildest horrors of the old Cantonese, and Mandarin, kitchen, such as live shrimp in wine and newborn mice, are now banned. There are still snake restaurants where you select your fresh cobra yourself from its cage; and a Cantonese store full of barking dogs is not a pet shop but a food shop.

7

EVERY TRAVELER IN ASIA was used to the good old Westinghouse fans in all the hotel rooms. They were often patched up and looking as if they had been kept going, grindingly, since Joseph Conrad days; but if their noise bothered a guest during his siesta, their presence gave him the security of knowing that the West makes things for the world. China's supply of Westinghouse fans is gone; perhaps Chiang Kai-shek took them with him to Taiwan. In the hotel rooms stand fans built in Shanghai, amazingly modern with all sorts of buttons and streamlined shapes. Radios do not sound very good, but they are Chinese-made too; in fact, it is well-nigh impossible to find anything in consumer goods which is not a local product. It is quite a change, for China used to import even its needles. The variety is there, too: barbers' chairs are offered for sale, electric hair dryers, bicycles, Chinese lutes, sunglasses, watches, pianos, hammers, drills, screwdrivers, flashlights, baseball bats, and even sten guns, believe it or not.

The cities have department stores, run by the state but again without that certain dreariness which for example Gum in Moscow shows. Most smaller shops are joint enterprises (half state, half private), and the tiniest ones are all private: the little tailors, perched on tables, sew and iron away into the late evening, like their brethren abroad. Ice-cream and soft-drink vendors have remained capitalist too. There are a vast number of them, according to old custom knocking on their boxes with pieces of wood and filling the streets with sound like a cloud of woodpeckers. The stores are crowded but rarely packed, and there are few waiting lines; in local terms, none of what they offer is cheap. The bookshops are packed with students; those who cannot buy, borrow books for one fen each, or just stand there and read. The big towns have "international bookstores" with foreign publications; the store in Peking had English editions of Browning, Milton, Aristophanes, Lenin, Stalin, Heine, and on one shelf stood no less that fifteen copies of Oliver Wendell Holmes' *Autocrat of the Breakfast Table.*

Any useful remark about how much all these things cost has to be wrapped in many qualifications. The exchange rate for the yuan, which is divided in a hundred fen, is forty American cents: a traveler arriving with dollars will receive two and a half yuan for each dollar. This rate has no meaning, of course, to the natives, and yuans cannot be exported. It is doubtful anyway that Pereira Inc. would give anything for them; they are not even traded in Moscow. A study by experts in *China Quarterly* (a British magazine) states that one yuan has 90% of the purchasing power of the 1965 U.S. dollar in commercial construction, 225% in residential construction, 150% for fuel, 45% for clothing, and 27% for industrial equipment. This is also academic; few Americans are having villas put up in China, and actually even changing a dollar bill may be considered a criminal offense by Washington under the Trading with the Enemy Act. So much, then, for the yuan versus the dollar.

But the value of the yuan may be pegged in terms of income. The salary of an apprentice in a textile mill, 35 yuan a month, is about bottom in the towns, and that of a senior physician in a hospital, 250 yuan a month, about top. Some idea of family budgets will be given later; it must be said now that rents are nominal, and that a food bill for one person runs to 10 yuan a month and up. Medical service is free for most, and since the government pays out the wages, there is obviously no need for income tax. All this has to be taken into account, for otherwise the people will seem even poorer than they are. A category may be invented, called the "Free-Spend Income" and which means: the income left after all basic necessities *except clothing* have been taken care of. This F-S income would then vary from about 20 to 200 yuan a month. A reasonably exact average would be around 30 yuan a month; 50 for a man or woman in a married couple where both work and where there's only one child or none. *One yuan, to 1.70 yuan a day,* then, is what the average town dweller has crackling if not jingling in his pocket these days (from 10 fen up, it is all paper money).

Against this background, here are some prices in yuan:

men's shirts yuan	5 to 15
sweaters	8 to 30
good-looking sneakers	10
little children's sneakers	2.60
leather children's shoes	7
cloth children's shoes	2
women's jackets, Mao Tse-tung style	45
women's shorts, in all colors	3
girl's blouses	3
good open leather women's shoes	8
good leather men's shoes	14 to 25
plastic sandals	2.30
leather sandals	8 and up
espadrilles	4
men's trousers, Western style	40
good material for a man's suit	20 for about a yard
straw hats	0.40
hand towels	0.80 and up
umbrellas	4
hand fans	1
suitcases of metal or wood	12
suitcases of rattan	10
big cloth suitcases with metal lock and trimmings	28
sturdy bicycles	145
those barber's chairs	240
big (professional) hair dryers	258
baby carriages (bamboo on wooden wheels)	5

sunglasses	yuan 3 and up
alarm clocks	10 and up
Chinese lutes	13
radios	50 and up, to Y 140 for three-wave models
a round wooden table on painted metal legs	10
a bamboo three-shelf rack	4
buckets	6.50
jerricans	7
pots and pans	1.50 and up
household tools	1 and up
flashlights	1.50 and up
little padlocks	0.60
toothbrushes	0.16 and up
combs	0.06 and up
soap	0.40 to 1
cigarets	0.20 to 0.50 a pack

In some big stores and in the markets, there are signs which give both the wholesale price at which the food was bought from the producers and the retail price to the customer. Chicken, for instance, was posted at 37 fen a pound wholesale and 42 fen a pound retail.

Here are some other food prices, written down in big stores:

lb. of apples	0.15
lb. of peaches	0.10

lb. of pork	yuan	0.50
lb. of dried fish		0.38
1 kilo eggs, about 20 (they are sold by weight)		1
lb. of rice, according to quality		0.08 to 0.12
lb. of sugar		0.70

Gasoline costs about 2 yuan a gallon to private persons, which is of limited interest since there is no pleasure driving; taxis are priced according to class. The bigger and shinier, the higher their class. A third-class cab in Peking costs Y 0.40 a mile, and Y 1.20 an hour for waiting; in Nanking, the cheapest class cab costs Y 0.50 a mile.

Bus fares are 4 to 12 fen. It's a very long ride in a pedicab (a tricycle for two passengers, with a driver who does the pedaling) which comes to 30 fen; their drivers insist on figuring out and paying back the change to the last fen. Some towns now have pedicabs with motors and these are not much cheaper than taxis.

Rickshaws no longer exist in China; they were "inconsistent with the brotherhood of men." They are indeed disgusting, of course, and can now be found only in Hong Kong; even Macao has abolished them (I am talking of the Chinese world). The Hong Kong Hilton seems unaware of any moral problem here; it has its own rickshaws at the hotel entrance, and on a pleasant evening one may watch heavy tourists there arguing over the fare with skeleton-thin, sweat-covered coolies. In the north of China, even the taking of pedicabs by able-bodied men is frowned upon; in Peking one sees them used mainly by women or people with luggage and/or children.

Hotel rooms in China, in more or less Western style, vary from 4 to 15 yuan a night. Those places where foreigners are housed average 10 yuan, four American dollars, for a room with private bath. Fifteen yuan is for a lavish setup with balconies and very modern or ornate Victorian furniture in vast arrays. The hotels inherited from the British in the former Concession towns have all the melancholy of long, dimly lit corridors, showerless bathtubs with rust stains, carpets in suicide colors, and that certain smell of an unaired English railway station waiting room. The others are quite nice. Laundry is very fast and very, very cheap (how could it be otherwise?), and a deluxe haircut costs 30 fen.

Long-distance train travel costs 4 fen a mile for a hard seat, and 8 fen for a berth in a semi-private compartment. A three-foot high metal safe, if anyone cares to know, costs about 400 yuan, and department stores display large collections of them.

8

NIGHT FALLS OVER HUNAN after the express has passed Chuchow. The Roman letters on the sign spell "Zhuzdjou" which is the way it is really pronounced; the bare station platform is brightly lit, and immediately afterward the little town looms up, dark in contrast. A few houses have lights on. It used to be not done in China, the people used to say, "Never light a lamp after supper." The train gains speed, its windows throw lighted oblongs along the empty street. There is a crossing, with a barrier, but no one in sight; and then the fields begin. The horizon is still visible against the sky where the sun has set, and the farmhouses are black spots. There is one with an electric light bulb burning in the door, then after a long while, one with an oil lamp behind its window. After that, all is dark. How does a Chinese peasant feel, lying awake in the night, hearing the whistle of the train going by? Is there security in the total familiarity of the breathing of his wife and his children in the dark, of a house and fields where he knows each tree, each ditch, each lump of earth, a man-made landscape like nowhere on earth, plowed and seeded for four thousand years by himself and his parents and his grandparents and so on backward? Does he still have the terror in his bones of all the natural and unnatural disasters of the past? Is he worried about his duties and obligations, or is he happy in the solidarities now demanded of him? It seems a new idea, visualizing a Chinese peasant lying awake in a little house within the endlessness of the land, and feeling happy. Who knows if happiness has been invented yet in China? The hills begin, suddenly; they rise from the flat fields with total abruptness, and blot the last light from the sky.

The landscape of eastern China has been worked over and worried over for so long, its weariness is almost tangible; nothing in it is incidental or unknown. Yet it seems wild and lonely in its remoteness. Remote from where? Remote from everywhere, from "the real world"—a feeling held not by travelers only, but also by the inhabitants of those little towns and villages. It is surprising to learn that China is the size of the United States; it has always seemed so much larger, and reasonably so: its distances were measured in human footsteps. Until a few years ago, a full one-third of China's prefectures could be reached only on foot or on a mule. The interior of China used to be a different country, and a hostile country; the government had no civil servants below the level of a county, two hundred to three hundred thousand people. Below that was darkness; only taxes came out of it, nothing went back in in return.

There were the old Imperial canals, used to carry grain and salt to the cities, silting up and almost dead by the end of the nineteenth century. There were no through roads. The railways, the few hundred miles of them, were built by foreigners. The first one, in 1876, from Shanghai to Woosung, was bought two years after its construction by the Chinese government, which broke it up and had the rails dumped on Taiwan. The trains, it was felt, had served no conceivable Imperial or Confucian purpose, and their tracks disturbed the harmony of nature as taught by *feng shui*—the art of balancing man, land, wind, and water, a kind of divine zoning law. The one most revolutionary act of the new government is perhaps its unwrapping of the countryside, its establishing of channels of communication between Peking and each peasant house—even if most of the traffic along these channels is one-way. And next to that, its leaving the secureness of the ancient provinces of Han and the Great Wall, and settling people in the naked, windy, lost new towns of China's Wild Northwest.

The industrialization of this country is now at that stage where trains and train engines are glamorous, where songs are written about famous engine drivers, and distances and performances painted on the tenders. In China as in many European countries, the railway workers have the oldest socialist and trade-union traditions: they played a part in every revolution and strike of this century, and they still cherish their corps spirit, their own emblem and their flag.

The new freight yards are large, there are many branch

lines that do not show yet on the latest Western maps, the Yangtse has finally been bridged at Wuhan, and a railway bridge at Nanking is under construction. The coaches I traveled in were all built between 1957 and 1964. They were very comfortable. The trains were always on schedule, though slow: they reach fifty miles an hour, which means a thirty-five-mile average per trip.

As soon as a train sets out, a journey-long tea drinking orgy starts; in first class the attendants bring thermos jugs of hot water, cups and little envelopes of tea; in third class the passengers must help themselves from hot water taps. Even a penniless traveler drinks "white tea," that is to say, hot water. The attendants also bring magazines and games, wipe everything, including the handles of the doors, at each stop, and pick up waste paper from the platforms in the unlikely event that there is any to pick up. These trains have hot and cold water with mix taps in the washrooms too, and even their toilets do not smell which is more than the Orient Express could boast of. There are, of course, the everlasting music and announcements in the corridors and compartments. (Westerners have reported that the speakers in the compartments can be turned low but not off; with years of practice in turning off the ring on my New York telephones, I silenced my speaker in a minute.)

Trains always halt for one quarter of an hour precisely, with everyone piling out onto the platform and making for the vendors of cakes, stale dumplings, slices of watermelon, and the same useless souvenirs travelers in a hurry everywhere are offered. A bell rings for the departure time. At many stations PT music, music to do physical training by, is played over the loud speakers; contrary to what one has been led to expect, this is mostly ignored. On my travels I have seen only three or four people do PT, and a depressing sight it is; there is something humorless about such public acts of self-improvement. Even a girl athlete team on one train journey, tall and pretty creatures in blue track suits, did not heed the call.

The dining cars on the big trains are packed with passengers most of the day (from all classes). They have real cooks working in these cars, men who appear on the platform at major stops and buy fresh supplies from farm women who come to the train with carts; I have watched them select produce and fruits with the care of a French restaurant owner. The guests in the diners make a terrible din, very un-Chinese as far as public behavior goes; for them too, then, being on the move has that exhilaration and sense of freedom which makes people forget their inhibitions.

Sight-seeing from a Chinese train window is most satisfactory. It means, for once, observing without being observed, no one to provide commentary, and unlimited cups of tea in the process. Views glide by, almost painfully allusive, as if arranged by an art editor: a little girl in a bright red dress, playing all alone in a vast, empty, green and silvery rice field; three old men bathing in a muddy stream under the broken arch of a brick bridge; a man sitting by himself on a little three-legged stool on a hill amidst a new planting of pine saplings; a cluster of people around a new irrigation pump, painted bright blue—they are just staring at it, and the pump isn't working yet; a young woman, in calf-length purple slacks, holding a naked infant by the hand, a hat dangling down its neck, and walking along a dike away from the train tracks, with no visible destination within miles.

The old is very much in appearance, the people treadling waterwheels, carrying loads at the ends of long poles, sloshing through the mud while plowing with a buffalo, and above all, the rows of them at the back-breaking unending planting of rice. The new is strewn in the middle of this, with no visible blurring of the edge, no visible influence yet of one upon the other. Factories emerge with heaps of coal in the yards and piles of machine parts, and high-tension wires; new looking apartment buildings of four and five stories stand in the middle of nowhere, or rather in the middle of paddy fields; a blindfolded mule pulls a waterwheel, two feet from an electric power pole; a coolie loaded down under a yoke with two wooden barrels of manure crosses without looking left or right a new canal bridge of prestressed concrete, in that same running shuffle the Aztecs (who did not have the wheel) used for their high-speed transport.

The train tracks are accompanied by telegraph wires, but rarely by a real road: only quite close to a city may appear a road of red, hard earth with a lonely truck or two. Whenever there is a bridge in such a road, another half-destroyed one still stands beside it. It seems as if every single bridge in China was blown up and rebuilt. And even the smallest paths crossing the train have barriers which the passing peasants themselves open and close; they stand there waiting until the train is gone, without bothering to put down their terrible loads.

9

SHANGHAI IS DIFFERENT from the other towns. Here is the mood of a big city, which Peking lacks; and Shanghai is Western—in a sense. The northern train stops first at Zhenru, a suburb or rather a satellite town, where abruptly a crop begins of new and old factories, mountains of coal, freight yards, semi-slums, old houses, and high buildings closing off the horizon. It is cooler here in summer, damper in winter, often greyish and gloomy. On a late afternoon, rain clouds chasing across the sky, with an early light burning here and there, and the mass of pedestrians (shoppers, and workers leaving or going to work, a few clutching umbrellas) streaming across the streets, it is like a scene from Zola or Arnold Bennett: a West European industrial town at the turn of the century. That is precisely Shanghai's heritage from its Western past. But the "proprietors," that species of men whose vices, bitchy wives, fat daughters, and endless meals Zola described with such relish, have gone. Shanghai is like a huge 1890 Manchester or Lille with the thin top layer cut off: it is a proletarian city.

Ten million people now live in the municipal district, six million in Shanghai proper. Of these six million, two million are students of some kind of other; one million are white-collar workers, and another one million work in industry with a blue collar or no collar. There are, as a matter of fact, still tens of thousands of "national capitalists" collecting interest on their former holdings, but they don't leave their mark on the visible town. The traveler comes out of the railway station—its vast hall filled with wooden benches on which people *sit* in line, waiting for their trains, rather grim and without that air of travel adventure which other Chinese stations have—and he faces Shanghai across a square. It looks impenetrable; it is teeming; puddles in the street and the low clouds reflect unseen neon signs; it is the capital of an unknown world.

Here, on July 1, 1921, the Chinese Communist Party was founded by twelve Chinese and one Dutchman (his name was Hendrikus Sneevliet, and twenty-one years later he was shot by the Germans in Holland as a member of the Dutch Resistance). It is not hard to imagine the inexorable stone and asphalt of these endless streets still stained with the blood spilled in all the rebellions and strikes and repressions. Whoever in his youth read André Malraux's *La Condition Humaine,* "Man's Fate," and remembers its mood first of fight, then of hopelessness, will understand. Both of these emotions still seem mixed in the very air of this town, although the lost battle, for which Malraux's hero was burned alive in the fire of a train engine by Chiang Kai-shek's police, has been won after all.

But like all towns which touch on water, Shanghai has beauty. The Bund, the waterfront avenue, curves along the Huangpo, an amazing river (called by Europeans the Wangpo in those days of Marlene Dietrich's *Last Train from Shanghai*) which leads to the Yangtse and the East China Sea. Shanghai is the first port of China, and of all China only on this river is the wide world in evidence. Which doesn't prevent children and adults from staring with a somewhat inimical astonishment at every foreigner ashore on the Bund.

The Bund was and still is one of the great streets of the world, like Fifth Avenue, Nevski Prospekt, and the Ginza. People stroll through the park at the waterfront, children roll in the grass, vendors of ices knock on wood, and young men take pictures of their girl friends. This picture taking is different from the Western pointing-like-a-gun approach: a tripod is set up, a smile arranged, all with great patience and care. Bystanders watch with neutral expressions on their faces. And while the posing girl leans over the stone balustrade and stares at the waves with a little smile, a junk goes by within ten feet, a man and a woman working a side oar with a furious effort against the stream, while a naked baby sits on deck, tied to a mast against falling overboard, and smiling back at the girl on the balustrade. On one end of the boulevard, where the street narrows and the tram tracks begin, the French Consulate General still stands, empty and boarded up. This was French territory once, the Rue du Consulat, Rue Colbert, Quai des Fosses. On the sidewalk across from the empty consulate, fishermen are sprinkling their sails with a tar mixture which has a foul smell and makes the passersby give them a wide berth.

At the other end of the Bund, the famous bronze lions of the former Hong Kong and Shanghai Bank (now the Municipal Council, with motionless soldiers on guard) which were taken away in 1949, have been put back. People used to touch them for luck; perhaps some wise official thought, "You never know." Little boys climb them and pull their tails, and bump into the guards when sliding off, but the guards ignore them.

Then comes the Peace Hotel, none other than the ex-Cathay of Sir Victor Sassoon; not far beyond there is, still, the British "office" as it is now officially called. Once it was the British Consulate General and the place from which Shanghai was virtually ruled. It is walled, but the Union Jack on its high flagpole is visible from afar—to the surprise of tourists who are told by their guides, "Two old English gentlemen live there." Actually, they are very young men, the British councillor and his assistant who take care of the problems of British and Commonwealth ships docking across the Garden Bridge in the bend of the river. Behind that wall lie impeccable English lawns, there is a tennis court with the net rolled up, and in the trees sparrows twitter in the great silence, while at the other side of the wall the throngs of Shanghai stream by. In the middle of the lawn stands a stone cross, commemorating the four men in Lord Elgin's party who were killed here in 1860. "That's why we burned their Summer Palace," the councillor tells his dinner guests. "Or so they used to say," he adds.

Forty thousand men and women work in the harbor which has a freight turnover of several million tons a month. Two hundred and fifty thousand tons monthly are unloaded in District Five, its harbor master says, which would add up to thirty million tons a year for the entire port; the officers of a Dutch freighter calling regularly on Shanghai thought that was a likely figure. "They're very speedy here," the Dutch captain said, "and terribly careful and honest. What really amazes me is that there are no flies. I never saw that before in Asia." When his ship docked in Shanghai, officials used to come aboard and inspect every cabin, look under every bunk and in every closet. "I think they were looking for drugs or arms," the captain said, "not for spies. But the last few years they've stopped these inspections. I still feel uneasy walking through Shanghai, they still don't like us."

Shanghai, in spite of its quick unloading and absence of flies, was not his favorite port, nor is it of any other freighter crew. It has a midnight curfew for visiting seamen, and until midnight there is precious little for them to do, anyway. They pile into cabs and make straight for the Seaman's Club on the Bund; when they come out again, all they have to do is mumble the name of their ship and the man at the hackstand, who has a list, will see to it that they're carted back to the proper gangway. Not that any of them is likely to come out of the club in a state of great joyous confusion. In its hall hangs a huge portrait of Mao Tse-tung with a text in English and Chinese saying "Workers of the World, Unite!" Well, there's at least some excitement in that, if it isn't the kind sailors come looking for. But once inside at the bar, the view is of a photograph of little girls swimming in a pond, with as a caption (in English), *Little fancies in swimming.* On the side wall is a large painting showing two Chinese servicemen coming home, welcomed by wives, smiling grandmothers, and chubby children. They carry suitcases and shopping nets and look rather civilian; the style of the thing is pure Norman Rockwell. Between those two scenes of bliss, it takes a determined man indeed to get drunk. There are no girls of course (any ladies sitting with Chinese sailors are definitely their wives); there is ping-pong in the basement; and a foreign currency store which sells marvelous bargains, including big floppy mink coats for three hundred dollars.

Quae mutatio rerum! Once this building housed the Shanghai Club, the most exclusive spot in the Far East, with a membership fee of £200 a year; an evening at its bar now—still the longest one in Asia—face to face with the swimming fancies, would be the just deserts for all who believe those stories about Free Love festering or blossoming under communism. The word has gone around now, and only very neophyte sailors whisper to the barman if there are . . . eh . . . any girls around. (The answer is that under Marxism-Leninism woman is no longer a chattel for sale; and that a good game of ping-pong will do as well.) Puritanism is, of course, as much traditional Chinese as it is typical of most revolutions, though on Taiwan officials still inform their visitors that "in Red China all women are common property." The Italian member of a trade mission to China, who had known Shanghai in the old days, tells everybody how sadly things have changed; yet it would seem one has to be pretty thick-skinned or just plain dull-witted to long back for that repulsive and sad hodgepodge of gangsters, refugees, and whores, which made up Shanghai's fame. The whores have been reformed; some of the White Russian refugees, by a bewildering spin of the wheel of fortune, are now respected haters of the Soviets and the teachers of Russian here; and as for Joe Kaufman and his Multi-Lingual Charm, to quote a prewar nightclub guide, he may be anywhere from Caracas to Jersey City.

The other pleasure spot of Shanghai is "The Great World," a five-story building with terraced walks and open staircases around a courtyard, where opera, film, and all kinds of vaudeville are staged. You pay a few cents at the door and are then free to visit each and all of these acts, to look into a funny mirror, shoot at pipe stems, or buy fruit drinks with shaved ice. I had always been fascinated by that name "The Great World" which has a haunting connotation; the reality is as depressing as any such place can be. A city official had told me with pride how its preliberation "low pornography" had been expurgated; making the rounds of all these moth-eaten acts it was hard to repress a bourgeois tinge of longing for just one sniff of such low pornography. I stood in line for a "What the Butler Saw" type of machine, but when my turn came, I found that one fen was needed to put in the slot, which I didn't have. The man behind me put one in for me, a most unusual thing to happen to a foreigner in China—not because of the friendliness but because of the intimacy of the gesture. It was my nicest experience in "The Great World." ("What the Butler Saw" turned out to be a set for a Peking revolutionary opera.) All this is not the reaction of a spoiled Westerner. The locals seemed rather bored and restless too, milling up and down the stairs; they were mostly children and teen-agers. My efforts to explain to my cabdriver, who had waited for me, that I was going to walk back to my hotel, provided them with every bit as much entertainment as all those floors of show business.

And what a walk that was! In the warm, dark night the sidewalks were sprawling with people, lying on mats, sitting on little chairs, children running through it all, in every state of dress and undress. Arguments, songs, conversations all added up to a curtain of sound which became almost a roar at a distance: the roar of a crowd ten blocks from the river and the sea, but as unexplored and mysterious as if they lived at the source of the Amazon; a crowd of men and women secure in their food, work, and way of life, but without-property—the Chinese word for proletarian is literally, "man without property." An unphotographable scene, too, for Shanghai does not take kindly to prying foreigners.

Ten minutes away lies the Peace Hotel, with its new visitors and tourists looking down on the river from the restaurant on the floor just below the top. That evening it had some very fat Germans who insisted on opening a window to take photographs, a quiet French couple, odd East Europeans in gay sport shirts looking like Yankees in a caricature in *Krokodil*, and then that vast body of travelers we do not know a thing about: delegates, experts, and students from the new countries of Africa and Asia. Once such men had to stay away from the facilities and amenities of modern travel unless they were Westernized; only recently have they been able to bustle around freely in a non-white, non-hard-currency, neither pro- nor anti-Communist, double occupancy to a room—world. They are a smiling, jolly, Rotarian type of men, with frail, mouse-still wives.

Below on the river, the ferry boats made slowly moving clusters of light, and lanterns swinging on junk masts were trembling red points. Hot, wet air blew in from the water through the German-opened window. The town was silent now; there was only the tooting of a ship signaling to its tug boats. "Quelle héritage," a Frenchman said to me, waving at the river, its ships and lights and cranes, meaning that China had inherited all that marvelousness from the West. But in 1949 the hatred of foreigners and of the foreign past of the city was so great that there were many men then in the government who advocated a policy of letting Shanghai, that monster, just wither away and vanish.

10

THE GAY OLD DAYS here, as we all know, were not just misery and exploitation; there was also a *douceur de vivre* (for the few) then, a certain color to life which is gone from a revolutionary and puritanical world. But surprisingly, not only do the old China hands know this, some of those puritanical and humorless government men realize quite well how it was. They are not just rejecting what they never knew, as their films and their writing show. And at this stage of the Chinese revolution, a film particularly is no private effort but in a way made by the entire government of the People's Republic.

There is as an example *A Life in Flames*, a film based on a fragment from *The Red Crag*, one of those multitudinous, popular novels, which came out a few years ago. The film is a big hit, a Chinese *Gone with the Wind*, and it is playing in many towns in several cinemas at the same time. Only the most expensive tickets (50 U.S. cents) are available without long queuing. *A Life in Flames* is fascinating, even if the nobility of the good guys becomes a bit much at times for the more sophisticated members in the audience. (The Chinese are no mean movie makers; they provide films for all the non-Communist countries in Asia.) It is set in Chungking, the river city on the upper Yangtse, in the last year of the civil war when Chiang Kai-shek was still in power there.

The film opens on scenes of the town during those final months: its glitter, corruption, spies, miseries, and hopes—so much in the classic Western tradition of great adventure movies that a Parisian, who went to see it at my urging, later said: "I expected any minute to see Humphrey Bogart appear." Jeeps dash through the streets, coffee shops are packed, fortune tellers and beggars are thick as flies, convicts and political prisoners unload ships at the river quay. From one of the river boats the hero of the film, a Communist underground leader, steps ashore. He is dressed fashionably in American style to avoid suspicion, and he cuts through the crowds, the tramps, and the policemen, with all the impressive disdain of the rich Chinese to whom such people were simply invisible.

But this image of Chungking during the last days of Chiang is not a propaganda caricature. It shows life as it must have been, downs and ups, including a big neon advertisement for Coca-Cola and a hawker with old copies of *Life* magazine for sale. Such subtle humor is indeed a rare item in Asia, and it is startling that the makers of the film had so much feeling not only for the sordidness of that time but also for its color and bustle and excitement—gone from their own more antiseptic days. One cannot help but wonder which Communist official wrote what memorandum to whom in order to get a Coca-Cola neon sign manufactured.

The only American in the movie is an officer, a political adviser; he looks convincing which is no surprise since he is played by an American actor, an ex-Korea P.O.W. The movie American is by no means a caricature either, and the advice he gives the Chiang officers sounds straight out of a State Department White Paper. The movie hero is captured during a café rendezvous with a traitor, and he is taken to Chungking prison which had a fame of its own in those days. Eventually, as he refuses to collaborate, he is executed just before the Communist Army enters Chungking. The music plays *The Internationale*, and some people in the audience cry.

That audience, at least in the towns, is quite sophisticated. There is a prison scene in this movie in which a newspaper has been smuggled into the cells with the sensational news that Chiang Kai-shek has resigned and General Li Tsung-jen has become Acting President. This occurred shortly before the collapse of the Nationalist armies. The prisoners draw new hope from these tidings. It so happened that I saw this movie on the very day that former Acting President Li—who took asylum in the United States in 1949—had come back home to Peking, straight from Englewood, New Jersey. His return was a solemnly announced propaganda victory; but when the movie audience saw his name in that 1949 Chiang newspaper, they broke up completely: a storm of hilarity swept through the house.

Chinese movies usually draw their material from that ample source, the "national myth" of the new republic. The Chinese myth is different from that of most other countries in being so recent; it is one part Japanese war, one part civil war. (Its American equivalent would be Valley Forge, Gettysburg, the Wild West, and both World Wars rolled into one.) This was the great experience of the older generation, and the government considers it a prime source of inspiration for the younger ones who, not having known the bad old times, might flag in their enthusiasm and self-discipline if not repeatedly confronted with these. The same subject matter makes up the new "revolutionary opera" which has pushed aside the classic opera. The triumph of the good guys (the Communists) over the bad guys (Kuomintang, Americans, and Japanese) is treated at length but not quite ad nauseam: these films and operas have more entertainment value than the dreary label, propaganda, might lead one to expect.

Good versus Bad is of course the basic theme of most drama, and to the audience it does not make too much difference who is who. The types remain the same; the blustering major may now be an officer of Chiang rather than of Emperor Chiung-chen, the peasant rebel may clutch a tommy gun instead of a sword, and the virtuous old lady with smooth grey hair may be shot rather than strangled; the characters are all there; the crooks and the dubious people are usually much more real than the pink-cheeked goodies; the overwhelming sense of continuity the Chinese have about themselves is not broken.

This audience gets bored too when the show is bad; when it is well done they seem to flock equally to classic and to revolutionary, or if you will, propaganda, material. That the whites (now represented by the United States) always have been and still are the enemies of China, comes as no shock or change; it is a lasting historical truth to them in which America's defeat of Japan was but an incident. (Have a sober look at a recent Western movie such as *The Forty Days of Peking.* No sane person in the U.S. has called it anti-Chinese propaganda, but think how it would strike a Chinese, or any Asian! The Chinese patriots are shown as crazy fanatics, and those who collaborate with us, the enemy, are the nice guys; the happy ending consists of the troops of some seven Western nations gaily marching into Peking. During the subsequent plunder of the town forty thousand Chinese were killed, but that wasn't shown. I remember my surprise long ago, when I saw an American movie about one of the Crusades in a theater in Djakarta. The audience cheered and applauded whenever the wicked Saracens got the better of the noble Christians—at all the wrong places, in short.)

There are still a lot of Russian movies making the rounds too, wartime quickies most of them. In these, actors looking very much indeed like Joseph Stalin, make appearances playing Stalin and gravely saving some desperate battle with the Germans. It has been suggested that they are shown to embarrass the Russians but it makes more sense to assume that they are shown because they were bought. They provide new linguistic experiences; one for instance, which I saw in Canton, has Russians and Germans all speaking dubbed-in Mandarin Chinese. Since the Cantonese have the same written language but a very different pronunciation, the speeches were also projected beside the screen in lengthy, vertical titles. To see and hear Stalin speak Chinese, with all its high and low pitches, as he discusses the front at Stalingrad with his generals, was already quite surprising. Then the scene switched to the German headquarters. Russian actors, playing SS officers, were contorting their faces and straining at their monocles with a will, but it did little good: the poor men had that slightly jowly Slavicness in their faces which seems to show a somewhat erratic easy-going temperament, and no matter how hard they tried, they looked neither wicked nor German. And here were these pseudo-German Russians, one more strike removed from their models, barking commands at their underlings in high-scaled Chinese, interspersed with "Heil Hitler!"s which were in German and untouched in the sound track.

There is a universality about show business; a Russian starlet having supper in the Metropole in Moscow looks, sounds, eats, laughs, listens and not-listens much like an American one at Sardi's. The "new Chinese," though very professional about their work, are different. They claim to be that most unnatural of phenomena, totally unselfish actors and actresses. They are more serious than any other intellectual or professional group about *lao dung*, the manual labor tasks for which everyone is supposed to volunteer, "to create class solidarity and to end the traditional Chinese contempt for manual work." The first star of the Peking Revolutionary Opera told me she was working as a nurse in a hospital just then, and was going to play the part of a nurse in the coming theater season (cynically, one might have felt that this *lao dung* was just the old Method raising its head.) "I've worked on the land, too," she said, "and hard. Now I am no longer annoyed when it rains, I now know what it means to the land. It is painful for an intellectual to remold his mind—what you in the West call brainwashing. But he is happier afterward. How else can we get across to the masses? How else can I learn to understand a peasant who considers human excrement not disgusting but a treasure?" She was a very beautiful girl.

She, and her director and company, had toured Europe and they talked knowledgeably about Western plays and opera. They said that East and West should learn from each other and influence each other in the theater, which is a heterodox idea in China right now. But they were self-righteous about their own ways of doing things, and contrasted their "team spirit" with the Western "dog-eat-dog atmosphere, actors fighting each other to rise on the ladder, knocking everyone else to boost their own stock." "That's how it used to be here too, in the Old China," the opera star said. It was rather annoying to listen to them going on and on, piously, about the mess in our theater, although they were probably right and the same things can be heard in the William Morris Agency or anywhere else on Broadway. "Our plays serve not us but the people," the girl told me.

"Well, so did Ibsen, and Shaw, and Chekhov," I answered, in as unpleasant a voice as possible, just to shake them up a bit. The director didn't stop smiling. "We know you have socialist artists too," he said encouragingly, "and we realize they have a harder time than we."

11

CHINESE FACTORIES did exist, but they were alien bodies in a country which seemed to live in a static and pre-industrial dream. They were built by and for foreigners, and were often no more than assembly plants for foreign products; and the country which had so many technical inventions to its name maintained a sullen passivity toward all the ingeniousness of the West.

This is in essence how things were until only twenty years ago. It helps to think of these matters while being led through the new plants on the conducted tours which are rather boring to anyone except an engineer or a spy; such thoughts give more life and interest to the enthusiasm which the Chinese factory workers seem to feel toward their machines. It is hard for Westerners to take the boy-meets-tractor romance seriously, or eagerly to pick up a magazine with a female welder for a cover girl; but the Chinese are in earnest about it all. To them, the new machines are no threat as they seemed to be to the craftsmen in the West at the beginning of the industrial revolution; to the contrary, in the machines alone lies their hope for a liberation from marginal living. To most factory workers, newly trained men, any machine is still a minor miracle, and to be in control of a lathe gives its operator an immense thrill of importance and power, and a share in the success of the machine, the factory, and the People's Republic itself.

This much becomes quite clear after a number of walks through these factories. It makes it believable that the men in the new industry, while working a forty-eight-hour week with no vacations and very little in the way of luxuries and comforts, may be contented men. There is no need to assume that they are more noble than an American or a French mechanic, or that they are working under wicked coercion. Those of them who remember prewar industrial conditions need little to be happy, for in the thirties men, women, and children were worked like serfs or worse in many places, locked up overnight between shifts, discarded when crippled or worn out. But of course there are fewer and fewer people to remember those days; and for the young generation the thrill of newness will wear off. Already on factory tours one comes upon men doing sweet nothing, picking up a tool or an oil can when they catch sight of the workshop manager—but without undue haste or alarm. It's a little thing, but it points toward the day when in China, too, new and private incentives will be needed to keep the people doing their work well.

Only the Northeast, the area we used to call Manchuria and

which the Japanese who occupied it for thirteen years called Manchukuo, has an industrial tradition, and although the Russians carted off most of the equipment in 1945 as war reparations, enough was left to provide a new basis. It is more interesting to look at a really new beginning, as for instance the automobile manufacturing in Nanking. The truck plant there had its beginning in what its founders call a "shoulder factory": the entire equipment was carried on the shoulders of the thirty men who ran it and who formed a repair unit in the Communist Army. When that army entered Nanking, these men took over an old building and set up shop first repairing, then building engines. In 1958 they produced their first truck.

Three thousand people are working here now, building 2.5-ton trucks with four- or six-cylinder engines, of fifty and seventy horsepower—figures of little interest since there are so many ways of computing h.p. The same engines are also put in pumps and generators. How many trucks do they turn out? No one will tell you that; "Thirty percent more last year than the year before," is the best answer one can get. On the assembly line one day, four were almost ready and it seemed a safe assumption they would represent one day's production. Several dozen trucks were lined up in the yard for delivery, and some twenty crated generators. The working conditions looked European-normal; there were plenty of large electric fans standing around in the halls and even portable air-conditioning units. If anything, the atmosphere was too relaxed; a German foreman would have been at these men with a vengeance. But the two supervisors who walked around with me, both veterans of the carry-your-own-factory days, beamed on it all like proud fathers.

They asked me, could I drive a truck, and when I said yes, they invited me to do so. This was a most surprising gesture in this country where a truck is a very precious item indeed, and where people don't invite responsibilities when they don't have to. (If I had hit a tree, they'd probably have been corresponding about it for the next three years.) So off I went; the truck felt fine, a bit rough on the gears—four forward ones—but with a good pickup. The brake was badly adjusted, but if they could build the thing, they'd be able to take care of that too. It had a minimum of frills, but it was not too different from the 1.5-ton Bedford I once drove in the British Army. "All auto workers learn from other countries," the manager said. "We copied some parts from imported trucks, but ours is a completely Chinese design. We use our own natural conditions." It seems unlikely that people would have sat down in the nineteen fifties to design a new 2.5-ton truck when there are so many fine ones running all over the world; but these statements are public relation efforts. The man who made them didn't carry it off too badly; he didn't quite give me a wink but he didn't overstate it either. Here as in the other factories I saw, no one said a word about Chairman Mao or the Party inspiring them—partly, perhaps, because it has been realized that Westerners just get restless during such harangues, but partly because the Great Leap Years have clearly been succeeded by a more matter-of-fact approach to factual matters.

In size and setup the factory compared to what they call a production brigade in a commune. In the same way as the peasants, the employees elected men to represent them and to audit the books; different from the peasants, they had no say in production management. The managers were of course appointed and given their orders by the state. All the people at the machines were very young; none of them looked over thirty. They averaged sixty yuan a month wages, and a third of them were women. Those were the most striking visual dissimilarities with a small European plant, all those young and unlined faces—Chinese seem to us younger than they are, already—and all those girls, in buttoned-up jackets and blouses, with prim hairbands, bending over their machines and looking grimly earnest, as if to make sure no one would not take them seriously there.

Nearby, on neat tree-lined streets, stood the workers' flats. The manager was very pleased with these and walked me up and down while an assistant, vainly and unnecessarily, tried to push various lines of laundry out of sight. They had a new canteen, and next to it a branch of the Nanking Bank. It was lunch time, and factory people were lined up at the two bank windows to make deposits in their savings accounts; very bored-looking ladies were stamping their bankbooks.

12

THE COUNTRYSIDE OF CHINA does not look so very different from countrysides in nearby parts of Asia, and the "production brigades" of a commune look very much like villages anywhere. As with the towns, this normalcy of scene comes as a shock, and here even more so. For though the Commune Storm in the Western press has died down and serious newspapers have reported that communes are not just a kind of production concentration camp, some of that image sticks in the mind. But if the split-up of families was ever tried, no trace of it remains. There is building activity, but it's farmhouses, schools, and many workshops, not barracks. The picture, assuredly, is not one of richness and modernity; for the handful of new pumps, there are still a hundred water-wheels drawn by mules or oxen or pedaled by peasants. For the handful of trucks, there are still a hundred carts, and men and women bent under their loads. The strongest note of newness is struck by the stacks of irrigation pipes everywhere, and by the tree saplings in the most unlikely spots. But many farm tools are in use which can also be seen in the Museum of Chinese History. "We are still very poor," the village heads say. "We are just beginning."

Their modernizing is organizational—that is what it comes down to. It does not show yet in the landscape. Communes, they tell you, are there in the first place to use, in joint enterprises, the hidden unemployment, the many days a year—a hundred and more—on which there was just nothing for a peasant to do. And they prove with a sea of figures how much more productive a commune is than a cluster of unorganized villages or even a co-op.

What about the web of rules and regulations a commune brings with it? "We had all sorts of point systems even before the Japanese War," one is told. (This refers to irrigation which, with many bitter feuds, was handled as a joint effort.) Of course the present system goes very much farther in laying down the law, and it seems to me that the vast new bureaucracy is tolerated only because of the honesty and incorruptibility of the new officials in it. About that honesty there is no doubt among the peasants, and a most unusual state of affairs it is for China. If ever the morale of the regime should weaken, this would be its danger spot: lagging officials. Communes may be more productive than a number of villages, but they are surely also more vulnerable to mismanagement.

Are they what the peasants themselves want? Perhaps people are happier puttering and even suffering on their own than being briskly told what to do. But it would be quixotic to brood over the "destruction of traditional values"; to be cured of that fear, all one has to do is to read for instance Professor Fei's *Peasant Life in China* of 1938:

In the Shanghai delta, 95% of the peasants were tenants; "in the interior, the yield of the soil is too low to make an attractive investment for the (Chinese) capitalists . . . it is reasonable to expect that, with the expansion of modern financial methods into regions as yet unaffected by them, similar conditions will tend to establish themselves." These tenants' rents, 40% or more of the yield from their lands, were regulated in terms of rice, but payment had to be made in money, and the rate of exchange was not the market one, "but arbitrarily determined by the union of landlords," who had police powers to collect. To pay the rent and the government tax, most peasants had to go to usurers whose rate of interest was "about 53% a month on the average." (Although according to an unenforced Kuomintang law, 20% a year was the maximum allowed.) The usurers employed collectors who "will use violence and take off or destroy anything at their disposal, and take children with them as slaves." "In the worst situation, the debtor may commit suicide at the house of the usurer," Professor Fei added consolingly. (Fei, a Ph.D. from London University, was in the 1950's a professor of sociology in China and had made himself unpopular by suggesting that the peasants should augment their incomes by engaging in trade; this was labeled "reactionary advice" because "trade is not productive, only increased productivity can help the peasants.")

The village which Professor Fei studied was burned down by the Japanese, but there are some new villages near the place where it stood, belonging to a commune spread out in that area. It is not far from Shanghai; pretty country, criss-crossed by canals with many sails, to Shanghai and the Yangtse River. I visited there on a bright day, when it was a pleasure to leave the smoke, bustle, and sullenness of Shanghai behind and drive out into a silent world, with junks sailing beside the road, and piles of red peppers and dark yellow sweet corn put out to dry right on the highway. I came to a village, spread on both sides of an arched brick bridge across a canal, and was received by the head, an old man in a white jacket, with a gentle face. There were seven hundred and fifty households in his area, one production brigade, and he invited me to pick those peasant houses I wanted to visit. After a considerable amount of courteous exchanges, we entered the farm he had clearly wanted me to see from the beginning. It was indeed nice, with two wings of five rooms each, two kitchens, and a little courtyard and a front room separating the wings. Here lived two families, an older brother with his wife and children, and a younger brother with his; fourteen people in all.

We were invited "to have a rest" in the front room, and sat on low wooden benches. It was cool in there. A man from the commune who had been warned of my visit, sat on the bench opposite me and chatted with the head man in low voices. A girl very graciously served us "white tea," little cups of hot water. I could see into the sunny courtyard which held a little tree, one chicken, and a cat. Across from me, in one of the kitchens, a very old man, the grandfather, was puttering around doing some cooking, dressed in a tattered grey jacket, half-long trousers, and his bare feet in slippers. The grandmother, looking even older, was sitting in the doorway on a stool with a child in her lap. About a dozen young girls from the village, some very pretty, were quietly standing in the doorway and staring at me.

Then we went out into the fields, and walked along little earthen dikes separating the rice plots. The paddy fields were the greenest green I have ever seen; rows of women were going down them with insecticide sprayers. Less lucky ones were weeding, which means bending down for endless hours. There were fields of corn too, looking excessively high, and along all the wider paths beans were planted. They met and made green tunnels with yellow flowers, and in their shade pumpkins grew.

I entered one more house, also nice, clean and inhabited by three generations, but declined a hesitant invitation to see more; it was clear enough from the road that most of the other houses were poorer and smaller than the ones we had seen.

(In spite of all those reservations about statistics, I have dutifully made notes of the production figures and tried to compare them with Fei's data for 1937, a comparison too tempting to be omitted. The commune has 31,000 *mu*, which is 5,000 acres, and two-fifths of this is planted in rice. The manager said they got 6,000 pounds of rice from an acre—in his actual words, 447 kilos from one mu—116% more than in 1949. The United States gets an average 3,650 pounds of rice per acre. That does not make the Chinese manager's figure preposterous, for they put in many times more man-hours. Professor Fei's mu seems to be an eighth instead of a sixth of an acre, and he worked with bushels instead of pounds. His village produced six bushels of rice per mu, but he does not say whether this was "paddy" rice in the husk, brown rice, or milled rice, which could make from 25% to 33% difference.

Assuming the highest figures all around, Fei's village got 3,000 pounds of rice from one acre. There was communal irrigation in those days, but haphazardly; the seedlings were planted wider apart; there was no alternation of wheat and rice, no machine pumps, and no chemical fertilizer. This may be sufficient to account for a jump from 3,000 to 6,000 pounds.)

I managed to get myself out of a visit to the children's nursery (which is like saying "No" to the question of friends, "Do you want to see our baby?"), and we went for a look at the commune workshop. These workshops are an addition to village life, the most tangible and perhaps the most revolutionary change made by communization. They are heirs to the ill-fated village iron foundries of the Great Leap; they are sophisticated little factories and not in the least resembling village smithies. Some have power lathes, heavy drills, metal presses, and various other power tools. They are bridgeheads of rural industrialization and in fact of modern rural thinking.

Peasants, men and women, are seen here repairing and building their own equipment: plow blades, rice-planting devices, pumps, all the way to new pistons for the village truck. Much of this still looks like not-very-well-directed tinkering, but it is soothing to observe these people with frowns of concentration on their faces, trying to figure out the mechanics of some implement or other—faces which used to have that blankness of resignation which does not instill pity in others but impatience and sadism.

Much is written in the Chinese press about "nationwide scientific education" and "scientific research," as if we were meant to visualize an entire country in white laboratory coats.

All it means—but it does mean that—is that these millions of peasants are slowly changing their vague, inherited, mystical thoughts about the world around them (in which, for instance, a plow of iron made the earth "sick") and entering a world of rational technical thinking.

13

THE SEA, in the deepest inlet of the Pacific Ocean, comes to within a hundred miles of Peking. That is the direction from which travelers used to arrive in the capital; they would come by boat to Tientsin, then by rented houseboat up the Pen Ho to Tungchow—eighty miles, and a two-day journey—and then the last thirteen miles to Peking in a springless cart, on horseback or on foot—as long as they got there before six in the afternoon, when the gate closed. The road consisted of "huge stone blocks, five feet long and wide and thick in proportion, but often worn away or clean gone," and traveling along it was "a considerable torture." The Japanese asphalted that road when they were in control, and the Communists lined it with trees; whenever there is a stable government in China, trees appear along the roads, and when there is trouble, they immediately disappear because the people cut them down and use them for firewood.

Now Tientsin-Peking is a two-hour train ride, and the line from Peking reaches the sea at Tangku, another half hour. But to get to a point where on a real beach you can dip your feet into the waves, the yellowish, lukewarm and mysterious waters of the Yellow Sea, you have to travel two hours more, to Pehtaiho. Between those two points, the railway veers away from the shore which curves undefinedly through marshes and salt plains flickering in the sunlight.

Pehtaiho is the best-known sea resort in China, not to say the only one known to Europeans. The British Ambassador Sir Claude Macdonald really put it on the map by weekending there on September 18, 1898; because of this outing the reform minister K'ang Yu-wei's attempts to get in touch with him in Peking that day to ask for help for his emperor were in vain, and as a result K'ang had to flee the country, Emperor Kuang-hsu was overthrown and locked up by the Empress Dowager, the Reform Movement came to an end, and feudalism was restored in China. Who knows how different history might have been but for Sir Claude's weekend? (It was of course but one of many instances in the annals of the British Commonwealth where the man in charge was playing golf or taking the sun at some crucial moment and couldn't be reached. But perhaps that's why England has come through so far.)

At the turn of the century, Pehtaiho was particularly popular with the Germans, and after 1914 the Japanese came in force and in the late thirties practically took over the place until 1945. Now some V.I.P. Chinese have their houses here, and there is a string of rest homes, sanatoriums, and children's camps. Half the beach is again under European occupation as a vacation area for the diplomats in Peking and the only place for them to get away from it all. They rent rooms or suites in a cluster of one-story summer homes on a low hill, overlooking the water; some missions have their own houses for the season. In spite of the great schism, the majority are still Russians and East Europeans, a new breed of diplomats: the men are hard-working and only arrive from town on Friday nights, they carry elaborate cameras and play volley ball on the beach; the older generation of wives stays in the shade and knits, the young ones sport bikinis and violent sun tans, and they all have flocks of well-behaved blond children, who tote as much skin-diving equipment and other gimmicks as their generation in California. All these goings-on are in a half-circle-shaped bay. On one prong of the land the fishermen of Pehtaiho dry their nets for their evening takeoffs, from the other prong classes of little Chinese schoolchildren, all in red trunks, are taught swimming. The only Chinese ever seen on the diplomats' beach are a lifeguard who mans a rowboat, and a team of no less than three girls and two men who appear every morning with a litter basket and collect the trash. There are two signs which say "Private Beach," but without doubt the Chinese bathers would stay on the other half of the beach anyway. This is beyond the fishermen's land tongue and also shaped in a half circle, with three huge white umbrellas planted on it, under which most of its visitors flock together between their earnest and far-out swimming bouts. Two signs, in Chinese, Russian, and English, forbid the taking of "panoramic pictures" and swimming in light bathing suits which are supposed to attract sharks, but no one pays attention to these rules.

The drive into Pehtaiho from the station leads through a strangely hybrid world of part revolutionary China, part Victorian Europe. The first impression is not unlike that of entering Saint Raphaël on the French Riviera from inland, the roads divided by the same green hedges deep in red hibiscus, the trees under a veil of red blossoms which are called Chinese mimosa, and the air filled with that unmistakable sensual South of France smell, clean sea air and sun on pines. Later the analogy fades. The streets of Pehtaiho lie quiet, and when a rare car appears, the lonely traffic policeman wakes from his trance and goes into some hopeful signaling. On Sundays, the women ice-cream vendors call through tin funnels to draw attention to their wares and also to warn strolling pedestrians off the middle of the road when there's any traffic coming. Young men walk along in wet bathing trunks, and a smell of cooking and of melon hangs over the two or three little restaurants of the town. The casino shows a Russian war movie and has loud music coming from amplifiers over its entrance, which, since not a soul is to be seen on its grounds, has an unpleasant effect. There are some well-stocked stores; recessed from the street and with their dark wooden walls, they look like godowns and one has to enter to see what kind of goods they sell.

In a little park, busts of Maxim Gorki and Lu Hsun face each other (Lu Hsun, an essayist and short-story writer who died in Shanghai in 1936, is invariably called the Chinese Maxim Gorki here; he was an original writer and the comparison does him no justice.) A flock of students come by on bicycles, clearly from a big city, and get off to buy ices. They are happily noisy and make a point of being unaware of anyone else. One of their group is a tall, bearded young man from Africa; they are all very chummy to him, but with just a touch of self-consciousness—as if this were East Hampton instead of Pehtaiho.

Quick thunderstorms pass over Pehtaiho in summer and drive everyone off the beach and the streets, and home—for there is really nowhere else to go. Then the guests settle on the verandas of their rooms and read, drink tea, doze, or stare at the water. Under the lashing rain, the Yellow Sea whose name right here is Po Hai, the Gulf of Chihli, becomes very unlike the Mediterranean—a wild, inimical sea reminiscent of pirate stories rather than pedalos. As the rain stops, huge bugs come out, monstrously oversized cockchafers which dash themselves against the windows and the first lamps to be lit. The diplomats' wives see with relief that it is time to take the children to dinner and they march to the restaurant which lies amidst the summer houses, the children carrying umbrellas and flashlights for the walk back later. In the restaurant is one central dining room, unpleasantly stuffy, which everybody tries to avoid, and around it a V-shaped screened porch with tables which is most agreeable. The food is served on flowery Bavarian china, originating way back to Pehtaiho's German days and having come through all those changes and wars without a chip or a crack. The radio of a nearby vacation colony can be heard playing *The Internationale* for what seems at least half an hour.

After dark it becomes very silent in Pehtaiho. I have walked there for miles without hearing or seeing anything but the bats fluttering under the trees, and once a young waiter in a white jacket who was sitting on the steps of a house and practicing on the recorder. A government limousine may glide by and turn into the driveway of one of the rather mysterious villas under the trees beyond the vacation colonies, houses built long ago by rich men from a vanished era. A searchlight appears against the sky, a reminder of the state of war between Taiwan and China.

14

TRADITIONALLY, LEISURE in China was not spent on any ocean beaches, where you'd find only fishermen, but in "beauty spots" which were carefully prearranged and man-improved. They must have been the prerogative of the elite, for no one else would have had time, or the knowledge of aesthetics, to dare visit them. They were reduced, softened, aspects of nature, and the rich carried this process even further and made gardens for themselves in which these famous sites were re-created in miniature. There one could sit and wander around a mountain in one's imagination—contemplation carried to a nice extreme. Now China has millions of new town inhabitants with new leisure even if it consists of just one day a week. Many of them have gone modern and Western and play ping-pong or go bicycling, but there are quite a number preserving a tradition by being just contemplative.

For instance, a young man who studies in Hangchow told me how fortunate he considered himself to live in "The Earthly Paradise." That is what Hangchow was called by the emperors of the Southern Sung Dynasty who made it their capital, and by the poet Po Chu-i who was a prefect of the town. Hangchow, now a rather sleepy place, a hundred and ten miles to the southwest of Shanghai on the Chientang River, has for the last thousand years been China's most famous beauty spot. Although it has a rather unpleasant climate—it is one of the "three ovens" of the country—it is indeed pretty to behold, in a ring of hills with the West Lake beside it. It comes as near as any town in China to being a tourist place, and overseas Chinese even fly here on package tours. But for these people, as for the happy student, there is very little to do. On the lake little boats are for hire, punted by lady gondoliers, but that is it. There is no swimming in the lake, and the days are long gone too when "singing girls" were rowed around and offered themselves for floating love, precursors to the Parisian ladies who slowly drive around in Chevrolet convertibles. Hangchow is a retreat within the world, a place where people quietly come to sit and gaze at a setting which is picturesque in the precise sense of the word; and those people include many of the young men in town who six days a week may study engineering and Marxism. The passivity of Hanchow's beauty becomes even more poignant because the setting was created by the silting up of the river. The lake was once a bay which gave Hangchow access to the sea; the river closed it up. Two of the most praised little coves in the lake used to be the busy twin ports of the town.

Every part of the lake has its own name, and these show the

literary character of the enjoyment derived from them: they bear such names as "The lake within the lake," and "The lake with the three pools that mirror the moon," although it does not mirror the moon any more or less than the other water around it. One day a year, the lake really comes into its own, on the festival of August fifteenth. (Approximately. Beside the official Western calendar, two others are still in existence, traditional lunar and traditional solar. The traditional solar year is divided into twenty-four periods, the beginning of each defined to the minute, and named after a phenomenon in nature. This leads to such poetic calendar divisions as Ching Che, "The waking of the insects," and Han Lu, "The dew is cold." The countryside still regulates many of its activities by the lunar calendar, which is ten days short of the synodical year and thus regularly needs an extra month. In this calendar, full moon is always on the fifteenth of the month.)

On Hangchow's moon festival day, lanterns are placed in three little stone towers which have their heads just emerging over the surface of the lake. Each tower has five portholes, which are covered with colored paper, and the pleasure of the celebration consists in observing the fifteen little colored moons reflected on the water, in a circle around the real, full moon.

But this kind of contemplation is not to be taken completely seriously, and relates to the real thing somewhat as a musical does to a Shakespearean drama.

15

THE FIRST SOUTHERN TOWN is Nanking, in spirit if not strictly geographically. (Shanghai, though farther south, is the ocean city of temperate climate, greyish and hard.) Nanking, whose name means "Capital of the South," lies at the latitude of Savannah, Georgia, and it has a touch of that same southern, feudal languidness. In the railway station there is already a different mood from the North, less precision and more warmth all around; the control officials are not just correctly polite but almost pleasant.

To arrive in Nanking from the north, the train crosses the two big rivers of China which cut it into three very roughly parallelogrammatic slices, the Hwang Ho and the Yangtse Kiang. The Hwang Ho is bridged; amidst empty fields it suddenly comes upon the traveler through the sharp clamor of steel on bare trestles. There is a farmhouse, then a soldier standing guard on a small platform, and then the wide, lonely river, with its muddyish water whirling around the bridge pillars. At night, a searchlight from the bridge is trained on it and cuts out a fantastic, turbulent yellow circle in the darkness. The Hwang Ho, the Yellow River, is indeed the color of its name, the color of the uplands soil which it still tears down and out into the sea. It is a tempestuous river, the curse of Northern China. A huge national plan has now been started which includes forty-six dams for the Yellow River, and canals to bring water from the Yangtse to the Yellow River and, through an aqueduct *underneath* it, to the dry northern plains. (Because the Hwang Ho carries so much solid matter, it has through the centuries raised itself well above the land around it, engaging the peasants in a permanent race to keep up with it in their dike building.)

The Yangtse is the second great divide, carrying almost thirty times as much water as the Hwang Ho to the sea (23 million gallons a second at its peak); an amazing river, traveling more than three thousand miles through one country, from the Tibetan high plateau to the East China Sea, and so navigable that in the foreign gunboat days it was China's jugular vein. As wide as the Amazon near its mouth, the boat traffic seems lost on it, the river tropical and abandoned instead of China's main waterway. It has been bridged now at Wuhan, with Russian help, by a span of more than a mile; but at Nanking only the stepping-stones for a bridge are ready, half a dozen caissons drawing a dotted line from Pukou on the northern shore to Nanking on the southern shore. The trains go on a ferry at Pukou and slowly steam—drift, it seems—across. And (to get back to Nanking), the arrival there is indeed as in a new country, it is a landing.

Nanking is at least twenty-five hundred years old; huddled amidst hills, heavily walled, and with the Yangtse as its northern boundary, it occupies a magnificently strategic site. Thus even more wars and sieges have moved across it than is par for the Chinese course. The Treaty of Nanking of 1842 ended the Opium War with England and started China's century as a demi-colony. In 1853 the men of the Taiping Rebellion of the Heavenly Kingdom, a peasant revolt, took Nanking, made it their capital, and held it for eleven years. Their leader, Hung Hsiu-chuan, a former schoolteacher and a Christian in a wild kind of way, had his headquarters in a stone boat "moored" in a pond; this *chinoiserie* (probably in emulation of a similar boat near the Peking Summer Palace) made for very cramped quarters, as any visitor to the boat, which is still rooted to its place, finds out. In 1864, with the final defeat of the Taiping Heavenly Kingdom by Manchu troops and the British General Gordon, Nanking fell after Hung Hsiu-chuan had committed suicide and peace demonstrators in Trafalgar Square (probably, in a bearded age, clean-shaven) had protested the English role in the suppression of the revolution.

Fifty years later, Sun Yat-sen made the capital of his new Chinese republic in Nanking, and his office just about a hundred feet away from Hung's stone boat is left untouched, too. It has a few straight chairs and a wooden desk with an alabaster lamp, and a wooden French telephone such as now sells in New York antique shops for fifty dollars. The rare visitor must open the shutters himself, for it is almost dark in there; but the old telephone is still connected.

Then, in the same compound in a more luxurious setting,

Chiang Kai-shek's former offices were housed. Here was the Kuomintang Palace in the days of the Japanese War, when, with Peking occupied territory, Nanking was once more China's capital. The provincial administration is now housed in the palace, and the flagpole in the courtyard stood bare next to a tall pine tree. Chiang has left no trace, but the concierge shows visitors the little gate in the pathway through which he alone was allowed to enter, while everyone else had to use the side entrances. (This was the only spot in all of China where I heard a reference made to Chiang).

Nanking's past has put its stamp on the town. It has a kind of faded monumentality which reminds one again of the American South in its antebellum glory. It has marvelously laid out avenues, with a central lane and side lanes for the slow traffic, and with double rows of trees between them. The sidewalks have shade trees too, and the overall effect is of a green, cool, and quiet park. The middle highway is sparsely traveled: there are the municipal trolleys, installed in 1960, a rare truck, and an even rarer car. Along the side lanes roll pedicabs, mule carts, carts drawn and pushed by human beings, bicyclists, plus an occasional flock of geese. There are traffic circles with central fountains, and shops all around them, and the major circle has the Sun Yat-sen monument. From there, one avenue leads east to the Sun Yat-sen mausoleum at the foot of the hills, and another leads to the southern gate and beyond to Yuhuatai Park.

The South Gate is called "the special gate," it is thicker than any other in China; it consists of five gates in a row, one continuing into the next, and creating a long, black catacomb. The traffic goes around it, of course, leading to a square with the bus terminal. From there, a path climbs the little hill where Yuhuatai begins. Its Chinese name means "Rain Flower Park," for here a Buddhist priest in the year 550 A.D. was rewarded for his piety with a shower of flowers, which turned into magnificently colored pebbles as they touched the ground. The Precious Stone Teahouse in the park used to sell these as religious souvenirs, and it still sells them; but now the stones are said to have been colored by "the blood of the martyrs." In Nationalist days, Yuhuatai was used as the place of execution for political prisoners—over a hundred thousand of them, the guidebook says—and the park is now dedicated to their memory, with the mass graves turned into a cemetery. Steps lead up to a stone column with the words: "The revolutionary spirit of the martyrs shall live on." Chinese monuments have an edge over ours in that their inscriptions are recognizably personal; this one is in Mao's handwriting. The pebbles are put on display in little cups filled with water, to make them shine to better advantage, and they are expensive: the nicest ones cost 5 yuan, which is the price of five good dinners. On a table outside the teahouse, second grade stones lie in big bowls and may be picked out with the help of a pair of chopsticks. Surprisingly and capitalistically, the income from this sale of pebbles donated by Buddha or nature and dedicated to the heroes of the revolution, stays in the pockets of the teahouse keeper. The park, full of flowers and wide lawns, is a pleasant walking ground, and in late afternoons a stream of town people makes its way toward it. Peddlers carry their wooden boxes of ices around, and boys sit at the side of the road behind tables with rows of glasses of tea for sale, each one neatly topped with a dish. Men are seen making their way with two covered buckets dangling from their shoulders; they look like East European pickle vendors but they carry night soil to the flower beds. (Every Chinese town has some blocks where the empty night soil carts are parked, dozens of them lined up beside each other; they must be scrubbed daily for there is no smell hovering over them.)

On the main streets of Nanking the ground level is all shops, lying in the dark shade of the foliage and of their awnings. The small ones are the most colorful, selling mats only, or parasols, or the big garlands of artificial flowers the Chinese are fond of; near the center of town, appear department stores with glass windows and neon-lit interiors, a restaurant, and movie theaters. Here too, hundreds of young men are seen on a workaday midafternoon, streaming in and out of the cinemas. One of the Nanking hits of the past season was a widescreen, color movie of the world table tennis championship, which China won.

Every now and again, a canal takes off from the avenues to the right or the left, and then there is a complete change of scenery: little rustic houses stand along these, with men drying nets at the water's edge or tending vegetable gardens. Another park appears, with a lake, a shuttered old teahouse at its shore (or perhaps it was once a temple), and beyond the water a peasant house amidst real farmland, and with smoke from a factory chimney rising over it; boys are swimming amidst the white and light-purple lotus flowers. Nanking is such a green town because of its many open spaces, which even along the main streets make unexpected grass fields; but these bare spots are all scars from some past war, siege, or battle; at one time the town was all built up right to its walls.

In the evening, every person in town from infants to very old men seems determined to get out into the air. Those who are ambulant make for the grass and lie, sit, have picnics, or drink tea from thermos bottles. The smallest children stand in baby pens in their doorways and watch the scene; venerable elders with wispy grey beards bring deck chairs out to the sidewalks and fan themselves with closed eyes. Families have supper at low tables in the street, perched on little stools or on their haunches. In the trees, the crickets start singing in vast choruses, their chirping rising and falling in precise time, led by who knows which conductor. The shops remain open, and their lamps and neon lights make bright lines and circles, among which the mass of shoppers amble, everyone neatly dressed now, some very neat, and some almost with chic. A few old ladies, with bound feet, hobble by.

Beside them, in a world of their own, as it were underneath the life of the town, go the drag coolies. All day long, men, women and children pull loads along the main axial road through Nanking from the North Gate to the South Gate; and in the cool of the evening, their numbers increase. They pull carts with tree trunks, with coal, oil drums, and cruelly huge rods of pig iron. There is a precise tally: a man alone pulls a load of three tree trunks, a man with a child helper five. One man, or one woman, pulls two iron rods, one grown-up and a child pull three. They walk in halters, with a rag in one hand to wipe the sweat out of their eyes. There are also larger teams, for instance four men pulling a cart with two cable drums, and they look in control of things and of themselves, chanting in unison, and stopping at times for a cigaret with a lot of shouting and laughter. But the men and women alone, or with a child struggling halfway behind them in its little halter, are agonizing: an old woman, a bald old man pulling iron with the veins standing out on his forehead, wiping his drawn face and only just at the beginning of the long avenue south, which slowly climbs upward—

(It is such an unbearable sight that I asked for an interview with the town manager, just to be able to discuss it with someone. "Their numbers decrease year by year," he said. "We are building trucks, but we still need them. We are trying. . . . Their turn will come. They're not because of the revolution, but in spite of it. . . ." He acted distressed.)

Empty carts, that is to say carts without iron or wood but with people on them, go by too; a cart with a sleeping child, a child pulling a cart with her mother asleep on it. And all of them have to go around the traffic circles, one ring of people pulling loads, and another ring of shoppers on the sidewalks; they don't look at each other.

Among the shoppers are quite a number of pretty girls and women; but also among the coolies dragging their carts are girls who are still pretty. I saw a ragged young woman one evening huddled on an empty cart under a tree, waiting to catch her breath. No one paid any attention to her. She had a face of pure, classic beauty.

16

DO THE CHINESE HATE America? This is the most frequent question asked of the traveler returning from China to the United States. There is something disconcertingly ingenuous about that approach—it is like the cartoon in *The New Yorker* which showed two middle-aged ladies asking their travel agent, "Where do they hate us least?" It puts America in the one-sided, passive, aloof role of accepting irrational like or dislike, in the manner of a Saint Bernard surrounded by snapping fox terriers.

American public opinion may not include hatred for "China," it does include hatred (or fear) of "Red China," and a weird dichotomy is maintained between the two. Washington's nonrecognition of the new government of 1949—then based on the supposed domination of China by Russia—has over the years somehow given reality to the idea that there *are* two Chinas, two physical realities, rather than one communistic China, plus part of its former government on an island in the East China Sea. (Chiang Kai-shek, discredited, had actually already resigned as president while still in China, but that is not even the point.) "Which China did you visit?" they ask me here, and I found that my daughter and her classmates in a New York school, seventh and eighth graders, indeed assumed there are two different countries in the world both confusingly called China. The bad China was peopled by Reds, a subhuman species; the newspapers reported the killing of (Vietnamese) Reds as the daily good news. In another approach, China itself is mentally cut in two: a government of Reds, and an imprisoned population who are on the side of the improbable Mme. Chiang and eagerly waiting for the H-bombs to drop on them.

The Germans with more reason had similar mistaken notions about Soviet Russia in 1941; there are surely not many instances in history (I cannot think of any) where the population of even the most misgoverned country, if governed by its own people, welcomed the attack of another nation. Moreover, all returning prewar residents will say that the Chinese are at present less misgoverned than they have been in a long time; and it is the very general impression of Westerners in Peking that nothing and nobody could ever put the solidarity of a Chinese, in any war, on the side of the white race. In China, "imperialism" is not an empty propaganda term; for every Chinese with whom I had a halfway serious conversation about it, it had a simplistic but precise meaning, viz. "white soldiers in a colored country." Townspeople, including some detached intellectuals, and peasants made aware of the world at large for the first time in their history, accepted this definition as it were instinctively.

Many Americans ignore the strength of such a bare thought or, rather, emotion: in American discussions of the Vietnamese war, it was rarely mentioned. Yet it seems obvious that the issue of race, so strong still on the white side of the fence, weighs very much heavier on the colored, underdog side. All of Asia, in a sense even Japan, has just emerged from a century of racial insult, the one insult no man will ever forgive. In the fall of 1965, the prime minister of Singapore gave as one of the reasons for his anti-Americanism the fact that an American doctor had once kept his wife waiting, that is to say, had given some white patients priority. Surely, a reporter wrote in *The New York Times,* this cannot be a real reason. Surely, it can. The enmity, or contempt, shown by the white race is an enduring experience.

But what then about Chiang Kai-shek, the Chinese ally of America? A man whose very existence depends exclusively on the United States is not a fine test case for Chinese racial attitudes. As far back as 1934, when he started his "New Life Movement," and later in his strange book *China's Destiny*—which, shades of Mao, was obligatory reading for every Chinese schoolchild—Chiang seemed to look at his compatriots through detached, Western eyes, embarrassed at their spitting in public in front of his friends, rather than at their poverty.

His government now publishes the wildest hate-(Red)-China diatribes and says it would welcome American bombs on Chinese towns; and yet even this does not gainsay a little theory hinted at earlier: that if there were a method to gauge a man's most secret thoughts, who knows but we would find that Chiang hates Washington and hates it more than Mao does.

Because this angle of "race war" hits men so hard and evokes such deep and unrational reactions, it is easy enough for the Chinese government to get the people involved. Like most Westerners, I was shocked to hear Chinese kindergarten tots sing about their determination to shoot down American planes (not that they looked as if they knew what it was all about), or see them act out their "Navy Song" which features a complete pantomime of warships at sea. An angry crowd, largely children, in Hangchow, who screamed at me for taking what they thought was going to be an "anti-Chinese" photograph, called me a dirty American and asked me to go back to Taiwan and to get out of the Dominican Republic. Many billboards have a poster on which a noble looking group of people of all races, usually led by a burly Chinese workman, take a stand against American Imperialism. The text informs us so; rarely do they show American soldiers attacking or being attacked. Some of these posters feature curvy and pretty girls with glossy black hair, clutching tommy guns; they have learned from the West to use sex in selling a message. A student guiding me in the former Western Concession in Tientsin told me somberly as we walked down Peace Street, "This was once a Japanese street. Then it became an American street. The Americans raced up and down this street in their jeeps. Many people lost their lives under the wheels." (I would have loved to answer, "Well, you should see Bruckner Boulevard on a Saturday evening," but such levities do not go over well at all.) In a more traditional vein the same student told me later, pointing at the former Italian church near the river, "That's where foreigners tortured our orphans," something he had obviously learned from his father rather than from the more subtle government propagandists.

But there is an important side to government "thought molding" which makes it rather different from what, for instance, the Hitler Youth was exposed to. Hitler was preparing a generation's minds for aggressive war. The Chinese government as of now seems to provide them with a substitute for war.

Through 1965, the Chinese heard daily how their brother nation of Vietnam was bombed and brutalized by the American Imperialists. In harping away on this, the Chinese government ran a risk: it confused the young people, and the newly politically conscious. Why weren't their great country and Chairman Mao doing something about this situation? If China were as powerful in fact as it is in the image created for its own people, it surely would have, but it is not. China will not be "doing something about it" unless it feels trapped into it; the Western and Asian diplomats in Peking agree on that. The Chinese government must be very well aware of the "preventive war" group in Washington, and of the fact that the American air force can destroy in an hour all that has been put together so slowly and painfully during the last fifteen years. But all this cannot be said. An outlet has to be found for all doubts and aggressions; words, resolutions and demonstrations must create an atmosphere in which it at least *looks* as if China is holding its own against the United States.

This seemed to be the mood, at the end of the year 1965. In every factory and commune, slogans were posted about "increased production to help Vietnam." Managers asked about these said that technical help was indeed going there; then they added that the main reasons for the slogans was "moral support." A theory would be that the issue of Vietnam was used to make people work harder; but the accent seems to lie differently and it would be nearer the truth, I think, to say that these slogans were meant to make the workers feel that they *were* helping Vietnam, even by just going about their business.

China's war of words reached one peak in the first days of September of 1965 with the article by Marshal Lin, the minister of defense, who compared the world at large to China during its civil war, and the United States to the cities held to the last by the Kuomintang reactionaries. Hsin Hua, the Chinese press agency, sent out a text in English. What on earth does the Ministry of Foreign Affairs think to achieve with this, and other similarly crude propaganda it puts out in English? Their answer is that these broadsides are not meant for "us," the West that is, but for the new nations of Africa and Asia. "If they were military rather than political statements," one Foreign Affairs public relations man said, "we wouldn't publish them; they would be kept secret." But what about the counterforce they evoke in the West? "We are not so naïve that we think Washington bases its policies on our newspaper articles." (A true Marxist official has to believe, of course, that history's course is preordained anyway. Whenever I asked an official if he thought that President Kennedy's death had made a difference in the development of the Vietnamese drama, he answered—automatically and dogmatically—"No.")

One battle in the English-language propaganda war is fought in the ether, for China does not jam foreign radio stations—the number of people listening to them must be negligible. All the good hotels have radios in the guest rooms; and it is strange after a long day in this very distant world to come back to one's room in the evening and hear the cool and crisp voice of a B.B.C. announcer with the Greenwich mean time noon news. It takes only a very short exposure to be able to place newscasts immediately: the accents are all impeccable, it is the choice of words which gives them away. Jolly and vague words come from London. As soon as the word "posterity" or "mankind" is heard, one can be sure it is Radio Peking; the B.B.C. rarely brings in posterity. Taiwan has lady announcers who try to sound Western and jazzy but whose voices and choice of words are too shrill. Worse perhaps than Peking is the Voice of America in its broadcasts to the lesser breeds, which it conducts in an intolerably patronizing, you'll-learn-yet-to-see-it-our-way fashion, clearly e-nun-cia-ting each word to make sure they all get it.

Just how powerful *is* China? Every Chinese man and woman between the ages of sixteen and twenty-five is a member of the "armed militia." This is a sobering thought, an army of a hundred million; but there is something to the remark of a military attaché who said, "If everyone's a member, no one is a member." The militia trains two weeks a year, often with mock-ups instead of real rifles; I have watched some of them at it and they looked bored and tired, for the exercise came at the end of a working day. The visible reality of it was not formidable, and gave the impression that the institution is there as much for the sake of political continuity as military strength. The senior members of this government make up the most homogeneous group of rulers anywhere in the world; they are all men from the Long-March guerrilla generation. The philosophy of a People's Militia is interwoven with their lives; it tells "How China was Won" and has now become a saga endlessly dear to them, from which they go on drawing support, comfort, and farfetched parallels and morals for the future. It is the institution which must keep the past alive for the present.

The Chinese Army and its arsenal may be formidable; it is invisible to the foreigner. There are plenty of soldiers on leave, doing the town in Peking and Shanghai, but they carry no arms and act very unbrassy. China has no draft; it would not have the arms and resources to train and equip an army of the size a draft would produce. Getting into the army is a prerogative, a glamorous job for which young men, especially from the countryside, compete. In the vein of Long-March nostalgia, the government in 1964 abolished all insignia of rank, which, however, is a mixed blessing to a private, for it makes most officers and noncoms feel they have to work doubly hard at acting and shouting like officers. In the old Chinese society, the military were at the very bottom of the social scale; and even now the (symbolic) soldier-hero Lei Fang, a kind of teenage male pinup and comic strip character, is a very unmartial type of fellow whose claim to fame rests on his gentleness and altruism. His alleged death came, not fighting imperialists, but in a road-building accident.

There is still another aspect to China's ranting and raving in print: the paternalism of this government. It is not only telling its people what to do—an old Chinese idea—but also what life and everything is all about. This is something new which no one had yet bothered to try; and what the people are told is that all is for the best in their best of all possible countries. Why then is their country met with such hostility, why doesn't the world at large, or even just Russia, do things their way? Clearly, all the others must be at fault, suppressed, ready for revolution. Uninvited to the party, China must maintain it didn't want to go in the first place. Unloved by the world, it must hold the world unlovable.

17

Lu Hsun, who was born in 1881 and died in 1936, was the great socialist writer of China. He lived in that marvelous stage in a country's life when art, literature and politics all flow into one; when young men talk through the night and go home through silent streets, feeling that a new dawn for their country and the world is at hand. A "marvelous state," that is, from a writing point of view; for Lu Hsun's life was one succession of exiles, fighting the censor, hiding from the police, taking refuge in the International Settlement in Shanghai, seeing friends vanish or executed, and eking out a living in some miserable job as a village schoolteacher or a translator. In his portrait with his short dark hair and a bushy moustache, he looks like a slightly oriental George Raft. When he died in Shanghai, ten thousand people followed his coffin. It was covered with a black flag, on which were the words: "The Soul of the Nation." Twenty years later he was reinterred in Shanghai Park under a flag with the same words; but this one was red.

Yet Lu Hsun was not a communist and certainly not a political pamphleteer. Perhaps he felt too hopeless for that. When a friend came to ask him to write for *New Youth*, the most influential magazine in the cultural revolt of the 1920's, his answer was, "Imagine an iron house without windows, absolutely indestructible, with many people fast asleep inside who will soon die of suffocation. But you know that since they will die in their sleep, they will not feel any of the pain of death. Now if you cry aloud to wake a few of the lighter sleepers, making those unfortunate few suffer the agony of irrevocable death, do you think you are doing them a good turn?"

But the friend answered, "Since a few have awoken, you can't say there is no hope of destroying the iron house."

Lu Hsun simply wrote about people's lives, heartbreaking short stories about their little hopes and miseries, and in them he did not expostulate or argue; he was a revolutionary writer in that restricted and at the same time absolute sense in which Dostoievski, Turgenev, and underneath their verbosity, Zola and Victor Hugo were revolutionary writers. He had a command of language which comes across even in rather businesslike translation:

> ... There was a rustle outside the window, as a pile of snow slipped down from the camellia which it had been bending beneath its weight; then the branches of the tree straightened themselves, showing even more clearly their dark thick foliage and blood-red flowers. The color of

> the sky became more slaty. Small sparrows chirped, probably because evening was near; and since the ground was covered with snow they could find nothing to eat and went early to their nests to sleep.

Those sparrows are as unforgettable to me as the most dramatic descriptions of the battles and the bloodshed of that time. And when, rarely, Lu Hsun theorizes, it does not disturb the texture. This is how he ends a story about a visit he paid to his old home in the small town of Shaohing. He finds a friend of his childhood, a peasant boy, who now, however, only mutters and bows, and calls him "sir." "But our children still have much in common," he thinks.

> I hope they will not be like us, that they will not allow a barrier to grow between them. But again I would not like them to have a treadmill existence like mine just because they want to be somebody; or to suffer until they become stupefied; nor yet, like others, to devote all their energies to dissipation. They should have a new life, a life we have never experienced.
>
> As I dozed, a stretch of jade-green sea shore spread itself before my eyes, and above, a round golden moon hung from a deep blue sky. I thought: hope cannot be said to exist, nor can it be said not to exist. It is just like the roads across the earth. For actually the earth had no roads to begin with, but when many men pass one way, a road is made.

This last sentence is now at times borrowed by the government for some campaign or other; but Lu Hsun was a man very different from the present generation of writers who turn out *Red Crag* type novels; a writer who would probably not be honored if he were writing now and perhaps not even published. But then it is not proper to try and lift a man into another era.

When I arrived in Hangchow, which is only forty miles from Shaohing where Lu Hsun was born and where he worked for many years, I immediately asked for a travel permit to go there. I had bought the complete English edition of his stories and essays in Peking and had been reading through these until late every night, till I began to feel I could almost look at China through his eyes. I was told I would surely not get permission on such short notice to travel to Shaohing by bus or train; thus I held out for a taxi, which would have cost as much as Lu Hsun earned in three months. On a Sunday, my next to last day in Hangchow, I finally decided to go and see the Foreigners' Police myself. Their office looked closed, but after much knocking a girl opened the door and the shutters of the waiting room. I told her I wanted to see the man in charge, and she said she was in charge. She asked me why I wanted to go to Shaohing, and I delivered quite a nice little lecture on Lu Hsun and what I thought of his importance. But she listened without a hint of a smile or indeed of any reaction, and when I had fallen silent, she finally said, "I am sorry, but it is not usual for foreigners to go to Shaohing." Lu Hsun would have been disgusted with such an answer, as I was.

Since he says as much about the old China in his stories as a slew of professors, and since it seems preposterous to write about a writer without giving him his own chance, one of his stories follows here; chosen not because it is his best or most typical but because it is short.

18

LU HSUN'S STORY OF KUNG I-CHI:

The wine shops in Luchen are not like those in other parts of China. They all have a right-angled counter facing the street, where hot water is kept ready for warming wine. When men come off work at midday and in the evening they buy a bowl of wine; it cost four coppers twenty years ago, but now it costs ten. Standing beside the counter, they drink it warm, and relax. Another copper will buy a plate of salted bamboo shoots or peas flavoured with aniseed, to go with the wine; while for a dozen coppers you can buy a meat dish. But most of these customers belong to the short-coated class, few of whom can afford this. Only those in long gowns enter the adjacent room to order wine and dishes, and sit and drink at leisure.

At the age of twelve I started work as a waiter in Prosperity Tavern, at the entrance to the town. The tavern keeper said I looked too foolish to serve the long-gowned customers, so I was given work in the outer room. Although the short-coated customers there were more easily pleased, there were quite a few trouble-makers among them too. They would insist on watching with their own eyes as the yellow wine was ladled from the keg, looking to see if there were any water at the bottom of the wine pot, and inspecting for themselves the immersion of the pot in hot water. Under such keen scrutiny, it was very difficult to dilute the wine. So after a few days my employer decided I was not suited for this work. Fortunately I had been recommended by someone influential, so he could not dismiss me, and I was transferred to the dull work of warming wine.

Thenceforward I stood all day behind the counter, fully engaged with my duties. Although I gave satisfaction at this work, I found it monotonous and futile. Our employer was a fierce-looking individual, and the customers were a morose lot, so that it was impossible to be gay. Only when Kung I-chi came to the tavern could I laugh a little. That is why I still remember him.

Kung was the only long-gowned customer to drink his wine standing. He was a big man, strangely pallid, and scars often showed among the wrinkles of his face. He had a large, unkempt beard, streaked with white. Although he wore a long gown, it was dirty and tattered, and looked as if it had not been washed or mended for over ten years. He used so many archaisms in his speech, it was impossible to understand half he said. As his surname was Kung, he was nicknamed "Kung-I-chi," the first three characters in a children's copy-book.

Whenever he came into the shop, everyone would look at him and chuckle. And someone would call out:

"Kung I-chi! There are some fresh scars on your face!"

Ignoring this remark, Kung would come to the counter to order two bowls of heated wine and a dish of peas flavoured with aniseed. And he would produce nine coppers. Someone else would then call out, in deliberately loud tones:

"You must have been stealing again!"

"Why spoil a man's good name groundlessly?" he would ask, opening his eyes wide.

"Pooh, good name indeed! Day before yesterday I saw you with my own eyes being hung up and beaten for stealing books from the Ho family!"

Then Kung would flush, the veins on his forehead standing out as he remonstrated: "Taking a book can't be considered stealing. . . . Taking a book, the affair of a scholar, can't be considered stealing!" Then followed quotations from the classics, like "A gentleman keeps his integrity even in poverty," and a jumble of archaic expressions till everybody was roaring with laughter and the whole tavern was gay.

From gossip I heard, Kung I-chi had studied the classics but had never passed the official examinations. With no way of making a living, he grew poorer and poorer, until he was practically reduced to beggary. Happily, he was a good calligrapher, and could get enough copying work to support himself. Unfortunately, he had failings: he liked drinking and was lazy. So after a few days he would invariably disappear, taking books, paper, brushes and inkstone with him. And after this had happened several times, nobody wanted to employ him as a copyist again. Then there was no help for him but to take to occasional pilfering. In our tavern his behaviour was exemplary. He never failed to pay up, although sometimes, when he had no ready money, his name would appear on the board where we listed debtors. However, in less than a month he would always settle, and his name would be wiped off the board again.

After drinking half a bowl of wine, Kung would regain his composure. But then someone would ask:

"Kung I-chi, do you really know how to read?"

When Kung looked as if such a question were beneath contempt, they would continue: "How is it you never passed even the lowest official examination?"

At that Kung would look disconsolate and ill at ease. His face would turn pale and his lips move, but only to utter those unintelligible classical expressions. Then everybody would laugh heartily again, and the whole tavern would be merry.

At such times, I could join in the laughter without being scolded by my master. In fact he often put such questions to Kung himself, to evoke laughter. Knowing it was no use talking to them, Kung would chat to us children. Once he asked me:

"Have you had any schooling?"

When I nodded, he said, "Well then, I'll test you. How do you write the character *hui* in *hui-hsiang* peas?"

I thought, "I'm not going to be tested by a beggar!" So I turned away and ignored him. After waiting for some time, he said very earnestly:

"You can't write it? I'll show you how. Mind you remember! You ought to remember such characters, because later when you have a shop of your own, you'll need them to make up your accounts."

It seemed to me I was still very far from owning a shop;

besides, our employer never entered hui-hsiang peas in the account book. Amused yet exasperated, I answered listlessly: "Who wants you as a teacher? Isn't it the character hui with the grass radical?"

Kung was delighted, and tapped two long fingernails on the counter. "Right, right!" he said, nodding. "Only there are four different ways of writing hui. Do you know them?" My patience exhausted, I scowled and made off. Kung I-chi had dipped his finger in wine, in order to trace the characters on the counter; but when he saw how indifferent I was, he sighed and looked most disappointed.

Sometimes children in the neighbourhood, hearing laughter, came to join the fun, and surrounded Kung I-chi. Then he would give them peas flavoured with aniseed, one apiece. After eating the peas, the children would still hang around, their eyes on the dish. Flustered, he would cover the dish with his hand and, bending forward from the waist, would say: "There isn't much. I haven't much as it is." Then straightening up to look at the peas again, he would shake his head. "Not much! Verily, not much, forsooth!" Then the children would scamper off, with shouts of laughter.

Kung I-chi was very good company, but without him we got along all right too.

One day, a few days before the Mid-Autumn Festival, the tavern keeper was laboriously making out his accounts. Taking down the board from the wall, he suddenly said: "Kung I-chi hasn't been in for a long time. He still owes nineteen coppers!" That made me realize how long it was since we had seen him.

"How could he come?" one of the customers said. "His legs were broken in that last beating."

"Ah!"

"He was stealing again. This time he was fool enough to steal from Mr. Ting, the provincial scholar! As if anybody could get away with that!"

"What then?"

"What then? First he had to write a confession, then he was beaten. The beating lasted nearly all night, until his legs were broken."

"And then?"

"Well, his legs were broken."

"Yes, but after that?"

"After? . . . Who knows? He may be dead."

The tavern keeper did not pursue his questions, but went on slowly making up his accounts.

After the Mid-Autumn Festival the wind grew colder every day, as winter came on. Even though I spent all my time by the stove, I had to wear my padded jacket. One afternoon, when the shop was empty, I was sitting with my eyes closed when I heard a voice:

"Warm a bowl of wine."

The voice was very low, yet familiar. But when I looked up, there was no one there. I stood up and looked towards the door, and there, beneath the counter, Kung I-chi was sitting, facing the threshold. His face was haggard and lean, and he looked in a terrible condition. He had on a ragged lined jacket, and was sitting cross-legged on a mat which was attached to his shoulders by a straw rope. When he saw me, he repeated:

"Warm a bowl of wine."

At this point my employer leaned over the counter and said: "Is that Kung I-chi? You still owe nineteen coppers!"

"That . . . I'll settle next time," replied Kung, looking up disconsolately. "Here's ready money; the wine must be good."

The tavern keeper, just as in the past, chuckled and said:

"Kung I-chi, you've been stealing again!"

But instead of protesting vigorously, the other simply said:

"You like your joke."

"Joke? If you didn't steal, why did they break your legs?"

"I fell," said Kung in a low voice. "I broke them in a fall." His eyes pleaded with the tavern keeper to let the matter drop. By now several people had gathered round, and they all laughed. I warmed the wine, carried it over, and set it on the threshold. He produced four coppers from his ragged coat pocket, and placed them in my hand. As he did so I saw that his hands were covered with mud—he must have crawled here on them. Presently he finished the wine and, amid the laughter and comments of the others, slowly dragged himself off by his hands.

A long time went by after that without our seeing Kung again. At the end of the year, when the tavern keeper took down the board, he said, "Kung I-chi still owes nineteen coppers!" At the Dragon Boat Festival the next year, he said the same thing again. But when the Mid-Autumn Festival came, he did not mention it. And another New Year came round without our seeing any more of him.

Nor have I ever seen him since—probably Kung I-chi is really dead.

19

THE "NEW MORALITY" is the most baffling aspect of the Chinese landscape. It is there, an essential trait which cannot be left out without the entire picture blurring; yet everyone sees it differently and some do not see it at all. Whoever wants to write about the country with objectivity will thus be tempted to skip it. Commentaries on China in American newspapers ignore it. It could even seem as if one of the reasons for the State Department's ban on travel to the country is the prevention of the study of this New Morality until it has worn off sufficiently—for wear off it does. This shows the chasm of our time: most people in the United States, if they think of it at all, think of present-day China as totally immoral, whereas China's leaders and their supporters are genuine in their feeling that their country is witnessing a triumph of morality on earth.

There was a physician in Peking who was one of the few Chinese to whom I had a direct, personal introduction. One evening I gave his address to a cabdriver and off we went, an unusual procedure for a foreigner; on purpose, I had not tried to telephone him first. After some circling around in a poor neighborhood, we found the doctor's door, I rang the bell observed by about fifty open-mouthed children, and his wife appeared and let me in. The house, behind a low wall, was unexpectedly nice. I presented the greetings of a Dutch sociologist we both knew, and then I gave the doctor an honest chance to get rid of me without being rude. But he did not. We sat for hours in his study, which looked out on a little courtyard, and drank (or in my case, pretended to drink) Maotai liqueur.

"I used to have a private practice, and my car, and quite a lot of money and leisure," the doctor said to me. "Now I'm a government employee and I have to work six days a week in a hospital, where I go by bus. But I'm happy because I never have to think about money when I look at a sick man. I have another purpose. I feel less free but more moral.

"How much more true do you think that would be for nine-tenths of our people, whose only freedom was the freedom to go to the devil? Our revolution was not supported by men who wanted to be left alone by their rulers, like the American Revolution. It was supported by men who wanted to be left alone no longer, but to be saved from the chaos and jungle our country lived in, and to be given food—and a purpose."

I am sure the doctor was talking to himself as much as to me and was not trying to convert me. I do not know how typical he is. Theoretically, the New Morality means that everyone works for the commonweal rather than for himself. In practice it is bound to fall short of that millennial recipe; but it has not led either to an anthill mentality where the individual does not count. The government's "care" for the individual, his health, education, and food, is overwhelmingly obvious to a visitor and confronts him wherever he wanders. I put the word "care" between quotes because it is a rather involved care. I am aware of the fact that each person is thus protected not for his own pleasure but because the country is the sum total of all these persons. Yet the government has tried to create a moral climate in which its citizens find their pleasure precisely in this knowledge that they are contributing to the common good.

Napoleon once said that it was cheaper to distribute medals than pensions. It will be argued that this morality climate is nothing more than a propaganda weapon, because it is easier to distribute morality than rice. Cheaper it may be, but it is not easier; it requires from all government executives an attitude that is little short of saintly. You cannot sell this brand of morality through the rolled-down window of a Volga limousine or from a carpeted office; in fact, you have to be as poor as the man you are selling it to. China has a New Class, but not in the Eastern European sense; its elite may have power but they have nothing else. It is a class of men who appear to be as puritanical and egalitarian as any follower of Babeuf or Saint-Just was. China is poor but proud, they tell the people, and we are all equally and honorably poor. How sincere are they? How sincere is for instance a government agronomist who voluteers for *lao dung* and goes to plant rice? Who knows? Do I.B.M. junior executives really prefer to wear white shirts, or do they do it only because they are supposed to? They may not know themselves.

This New Class of cadres works through persuasion rather than force, although this persuasion—like most concepts about China—needs qualification. The need to conform is as old as Chinese society, in which for instance widows frequently committed suicide rather than remarry, under the pressure of what was *then* accepted morality. Stalin had nothing like that to take the place of his camps. The appeal to puritanism continues a tradition of self-discipline not unlike that taught by Confucius. Finally, there is this thing called "national pride" which has not had much of a chance in China since 1840; here again it is different from the communist countries of Europe. Even the rich and the upper middle class of Chinese were plebs in the eyes of the most vulgar nose-picking shipping clerk fresh from Europe; and their rehabilitation in this particular respect compensates them at least to a degree for the comforts they, and only they, lost. For everyone else it is a bonus. After a century which enlivened this country with six major rebellions or revolutions, two civil wars, five wars involving every single world power, and one war of annihilation waged on it by Japan, it seems to be trying to find itself again, using communism for its purpose; and this communism is real communism but it also is really Chinese. How wrong were those who thought that the Chinese Communists were just some kind of rural reformers; but how equally wrong were they who told us that China was not using communism but that "International Communism" with its H.Q. in Moscow was using China.

Outwardly and at first sight, this more or less communistic society looks very normal and usual to the Westerner; after a while the most contrasting characteristic to emerge is precisely what that Peking doctor hammered on: its moneylessness.

Not its poverty, but the fact that money as such plays such a minor role. This is perhaps an unpleasant situation for the rich foreigner (that is to say, any foreigner), who ponders how he would feel in it; but it is hard to argue that it is less moral than our society.

Here is a world in which relationships of work, profession, and business are not steered by the classical rules of profit and economy; thus other disciplinary and steering forces are needed to make it function. The sum of these forces make up the New Morality. One: every Chinese must be fed, housed clothed and educated *because* he is Chinese, and he must be his (Chinese) brother's keeper; and two: every Chinese must work as well as he can for his country. Propositions One and Two are parallel; Number Two is supposedly not pursued to provide for Number One. This society is non-economic and vastly experimental, a quality passed over by those who discuss Mao as if he were only a latter-day Kublai Khan.

Perhaps we had something reminiscent of it in the Middle Ages before the rise of early capitalism, when custom and Christianity provided the rules. Perhaps we should not even talk about capitalism versus communism but about a "money society" versus a "rules society." Such a rules society would function best in isolation, and the intense isolation of China, imposed on it by the United States since 1949 and by the U.S.S.R. since 1959, paradoxically creates the right climate for its drastically different character. In this atmosphere, it isn't so strange or unbelievable any more that government tax collectors became incorruptible, that waiters *really* don't want tips, that a lost wallet is always brought back, that doors do not have to be locked, and that some intellectuals want to prove that they no longer feel contempt for peasants by lugging buckets of manure in their free time. The pat answers of people, questioned about their wishes for the future, that they'll do what's best for everyone, become less annoyingly smug and less unreal; it becomes conceivable that at least some of them mean it.

What happens to the voices of dissent in this very particular society? They have no chance; in a sense they are sacrificed. That does not mean that a majority of the population of China is against the revolution. "Why then," asks the visitor, "hasn't China, has no country like China, ever had a real election, which would prove this?"

Paraphrasing many comments on this, the answer of the Chinese politicians would seem to be that "the demands which the revolution makes on the people are too intense to admit the doubt of choice." "If we open the doors, people would go in all directions, and the revolution would perish. Western economy, or democracy, seems to us to be based on the fact that man is bad, totally selfish. Accepting this, you try to make your society work without appealing to man's morality.

"This is a bleak assumption. We want to think that our people are finally going to be better-than-they-ought-to-be, that they can be made ready for the brotherhood of man; but only if we show them we are totally sure of what we are doing, will they accept the discipline. They have to be made to, because they are weak. . . . In Russia, they are already drifting back to the old ways" (I am translating freely). . . . "We will not let them. That is what *lao dung* is about, everyone having a hand at all work, talking to, eating with, living with the masses." (The Chinese love to make numerical programs of this type.)

Is all this true? Does this regime act through oppression

since it invades people's privacy, or is it breaking through old walls of egoism and showing them a new chance—in the conditions of China, perhaps their only chance? Which is true, the black or the white? But both, of course, and both at the same time!

That is why the repeated questions, "But were people free to talk?," "Did you see the opposition?" are so much not of the essence. Of course people are not "free to talk." Of course a former landlord may hate the Communists without being able to talk about it to anyone. The fact that his feelings are unsaid is part of the picture of the revolution. If this landlord would go to Hong Kong and there talk freely, this freedom (also relative, tilted by new circumstances) would not throw any new light on events.

The most dangerous lack of freedom is perhaps in the Western beholder. He has to work so hard—once the initial shock of newness has worn off—not to return slowly but surely to the tracks of his own, pro or anti, prejudices. All this is no sophistic argument in any direction: the program of the Chinese government is clearly imposed upon its people, not by force, but by forceful persuasion. It is completely up to the beholder to give this action its label.

But as the West rebelled against a pure money society and voted itself labor laws and social security, thus there seems to be in the air already a Chinese tiredness with virtue being its own reward, and a hankering after rewards more base but more directly enjoyable. Most men are frustrated idealists; given the proper reasons, they will work twice as hard, eat half as much, and be happy in the process. In the West we rediscover these truths only while serving in a World War; we then also discover that this feeling does not last. In China it will not last either. It seems to have reached one high just before the Great Leap, when the initial successes in reconstruction of the country and the continued (and to most Chinese well-nigh unbelievable) integrity of the officials combined to make many feel that their government could bring about almost anything if they just wanted it enough. There are, for instance, ample documents available which show that in those days, indeed, large numbers of peasants combined of their own accord into communes.

Since then things have calmed down. Villagers are amused when they receive a Red Banner, but they also want to raise their own pigs. A reaction is here. Now editorials argue that everyone needs eight hours' sleep, that political meetings should not take up a man's free time, and that it is not wrong to buy a bowl with goldfish—the traditional Chinese symbol of detached leisure.

All this may make China a more "normal" country in the long run, easier to get along with; and it is therefore a Good Thing. But its period of exhilaration is worth studying with an open mind, even if it was, or is, or seems to be, a threat to the West. Mankind's exhilarations are few and far between.

20

MOST CHINESE NAMES as given by our maps (even sensible maps like Bartholomew's, printed in Edinburgh, the best now available on China) will not evoke a glimmer of recognition on the face of a Chinese train conductor, or of anyone else here. This is because English transliteration of Chinese names is so far off the mark, and gives us little idea of the names-world the Chinese live in. Asking for "Peking" will not get across that we are thinking of a town pronounced "Bay-jing," and "Nanking" is not close enough to "Nanjing." Canton is hopelessly off: the place is really called "Guangjoe." Since most people buy maps for traveling in a country and not to bomb it, this situation seems regrettable. One of the reasons the various systems of Romanization of Chinese do not work is that Mr. Wade and other Englishmen who worked on this, frequently used the pronunciation of the Canton area, where the first foreigners lived, and which is totally different from official, "Mandarin" Chinese. (In the case of Canton, the name of the province, Kwangtung, Kantun, was moreover mistaken for the name of the town.) The Russian system of transliteration, created by an eighteenth-century church mission sent by Czar Peter, and which arrived in North China, is very much better, although their "Pekin" is wrong too.

If we wanted to be sensible (a big if), we could without effort switch to a well-nigh perfect Roman phonetic alphabet of twenty-six letters and four accents for pitch, now designed by the Chinese themselves. Names of towns in railway stations, names of major streets, and even of many offices and stores are at present posted in Roman letters underneath the Chinese ideographs, and all school children learn to use them during the first two years of grade school. This is a tiny first step toward alphabetization of the language.

Such an alphabetization of the ideographic script, in which each word, at least originally, is written as a different character, is so complicated because the Chinese written language is the only link between a dozen different forms of spoken Chinese. A Cantonese cannot understand a man from Peking, and a Peking movie needs subtitles everywhere else in the country: subtitles simply of written Chinese which all audiences can read but all pronounce differently. Even a Japanese can read it, and one sees Japanese tourists in restaurants write out their requests to the waiter with one finger, in the air or in the palm of their hand. A good parallel are our numerals which all nations can read but which they all voice in their own ways. Thus the first step toward simplification of the Chinese script, which hangs like an albatross around the necks of engineers, teachers, writers and scientists, is to introduce everywhere the official pronunciation, that of Peking, in the hope that it will eventually supersede the local spoken languages which are called *pai hua*, "white tongues," because they remain unwritten. This is what the Roman phonetic alphabet is for.

In the meantime, work by a state council has been going on to simplify the Chinese characters themselves. This is a snail-pace process too, for the simplified characters must still be understood by those who learned only the old ones. About five hundred have been adopted so far; some by substituting the print character for the handwritten italic, if it was simpler, others by leaving out strokes if it could be done without confusion. "Literacy" consists of knowing two thousand characters, and that is enough to read the big newspapers which use a basic jargon that leaves little room for subtleties. The Western popular press does the same, of course, but this goes much farther; and a man who has just learned to read the *People's Daily* cannot make much of the crime news or the gossip column in a Hong Kong Chinese paper which uses terms never found in the communist dailies.

A serious novel or a technical book will use up to ten thousand characters; and in the entire body of Chinese writing there are some seventy thousand different ones; of course no one comes near knowing them all. Worse is that there is no such thing as a Chinese real typewriter, that all books and newspapers have to be set by hand, with two thousand characters an hour the national speed record, and that teletype communications and such present staggering problems. (Churchill suggests in his war memoirs that it was that kind of communication problem which made the Japanese Navy so inferior to the American in improvisation during battle.)

Traditionally, in Chinese grade schools the only thing children learned during six years was reading and writing; now they have added arithmetic, music, geography and the other standard Western subjects. Elementary education has been made almost universal; the school people say that the young and middle-aged in the towns are now all literate. This is quite a claim in a country which was 90% or more illiterate; but it is easily checked and looks true enough. I never came upon anyone, not even the raggiest pedicab driver or eat-house table swiper, who could not read and write. To see a poor working man in Asia handle a pencil and paper used to be a most unnatural spectacle indeed.

China produces three billion words a year in books, newspapers and magazines, of which at most twenty million are translated into any Western language. There must be a lot of repetitiveness in that three billion words outpour, but we certainly are missing much too. Several American universities, and I.B.M., work on programs of computer translation, the only way to make a dent in all this material. I have read samples from a computer already in use, which stores 6,500 characters plus a vast amount of linguistic peculiarities and usages; its style is far from splendid but it gives the idea of the text it translates.

In fact, its English sounds a lot like that of a new generation of interpreters in China, young men who have gone through a one- or two-year cram course based mainly on books. "I am emphasized by his running spirit," one of them said once during a discussion, and this meant: "I'm impressed by his fast mind."

Russian has been replaced by English as second language in the schools; a major change which may be the most cheerful item of foreign policy to come out of China in the last few years. At least there will be more possibility of conversation and—comparable to a sale of machines creating a future market for spare parts—the introduction of a language paves the way for some philosophies inherent in it. There is more to translating than substituting one word for another; every thought and idea changes color in translation. Language, of course, shapes people, just as people shape their language. China has started recruiting teachers of English from England and also from Holland and France, on a large scale and with a minimum of red tape; two-year contracts are offered to anyone with some college education at £800 a year and with no questions asked about his politics or anything else.

An overwhelming amount of work is facing the still small group of Chinese language students: translation of entire Western technical libraries, interpreting for almost every foreigner who enters the country. (Some of these interpreters are marvelous, some are terrible; and although these are all chosen young men considered able to handle their contacts with the wicked West, they are as different as students anywhere. The best one I met was a very young and unpleasant student in Peking. He could whisper a complete simultaneous translation in one's ear during a play or movie, but he used to lecture me on the meaning of what he interpreted, until I told him that I had read Marx before he was born, and would he please stop it; thereafter he never volunteered another word. The worst one I worked with was a student in Shanghai, whom I had engaged for a complicated technical talk with a professor there. He understood neither my questions nor the professor's answers, and we ended up in a general melee in which we both tried to explain to the interpreter what it was all about. It seemed an infuriating waste of an opportunity, but before I had a chance to start complaining about him, I suddenly noticed that he had prepared a long list of technical terms in Chinese and English, which he kept peering at like a cheating schoolboy. Because of the timing of the meeting, he couldn't possibly have made his list except during the preceding night. He was a very frail and sad-looking creature; there was something ill-organized about him which reminded one of Cantinflas.)

21

DAILY LIFE IN CHINA for, say, a young girl working in the Peking Knitting and Weaving Factory, means tending a machine loom or cutting patterns from six in the morning until half past two in the afternoon, with a half-hour lunch break in the canteen. That is, if she is on the first shift, which is the most desired one. The other two are from 2:30 P.M. to 11 P.M. and from 11 P.M. to 6 A.M. Her factory has two thousand workers, half of them women, average age thirty, and it produces coats, jackets, trousers, underwear, and baby clothes. If the girl is a beginner, she will earn about thirty-five yuan a month, with the usual social benefits, and will get her clothes cheap; some of the things made are quite fashionable, such as spring coats in gay colors and underwear of nylon or something akin to it.

Where does she go at half past two in the afternoon? If she lives in town with parents or relatives, she'll get to Peking on a bus, a modern one, with automatic doors and no one hanging on outside in the customary Asian style; the service is well-run, there'll be a bus along every ten minutes and the entire route is posted on signs at each stop. If she has been saving, she may already have bought herself a bicycle and use that; it is a thirty-minute ride to the heart of town, along quiet streets, with newly planted trees, not more than ten feet high yet.

If she has no parents in Peking and belongs to the six hundred people of the personnel living in factory housing, she'll just cross the road and go to her room. Being young and unmarried, she'll live in a dormitory room which she shares with three other girls and for which the rent is something like one yuan a month. They'll all four be on the same shift, and they may now close the curtains and have a nap, or do their laundry and sewing, or drink tea and chat. The room contains nothing but four beds, the girls' suitcases, two chairs, and a lightbulb with a little paper shade. It is scrubbed clean, and the care spent on making it look cosy without spending money (strips of colored paper, photographs and pictures cut from magazines all over the walls, a glass jar with a sprig or some flowers) is almost painful to an onlooker. The building has a bathroom on each floor with a sink, shower, and flush toilet, but no kitchens, and the girl will have her dinner in the factory canteen too.

But once in a while she'll eat in a restaurant, even with a boy friend perhaps—not just the two of them, but a group of four or six. She will also be able to afford a movie (or a play) once a week, a real movie, that is. Tickets for all kinds of instructive and documentary events are offered free by the factory, but pressure to attend that kind of thing has stopped in the past few years. Once a week there will be a political meeting though, or a union gathering, where factory policies are discussed and people singled out for praise or blame. If she has had an education, she will fill many hours reading library books, but if she never finished grade or high school, she will probably go to the classes run by the factory for people like her with part-time and full-time teachers. If she has no such ambitions, she can sit in the factory's TV room, or play ping-pong. In either case, she will be in a study group of the writings of Chairman Mao. They'll meet and sit in the grass, or in winter in some commons room, and take turns in reading aloud his little essays on life, art, dialectics, guerrilla warfare, the need for education, the relation between knowing and doing, and most other subjects imaginable.

In summer (when it will be suffocating in the dormitory), she can go swimming in a nearby pool for five fen. She works six days a week; as a rule she'll have Sunday off, but there is a stagger system and occasionally it may be another day. There is no vacation except for visiting parents or relatives living elsewhere. She may volunteer for a month of work on the land, which young people often do for the adventure as much as for any other reason. If she has already acquired some factory skill, she will possibly be told her work is of more value to the country where she is; on the other hand, if she is quite expendable, she may be asked to go for a whole year.

There are numerous hairdressers in her town, and she has been assured in various recent editorials that there is nothing uncommunistic in having her hair done, or in saving money for fitted slacks, high-heeled shoes, or even a "bourgeois" wedding. Sales and bargains are advertised in the newspapers and on slides in the movie houses; but most advertisements are directed at enterprises, and concern such items as engines or cement pipes. At her weekly movie, she will also be exposed to government slides that ask her to learn swimming but not to bathe in rivers or the sea all by herself, and not to read too late in bed or under a street light: "Save your eyes for your country."

During her morning work, there'll be a tea break and music to do exercises by in the courtyard, but if she is typical she will just sit on the edge of a work table and sip her tea. If she's very modern, she may even smoke a cigaret. There will be factory outings which, at her age, she'll join very eagerly. They may have buses, but they may also just have to sit on wooden benches, or stand, on open trucks. They'll sing and be very excited all the same. (Most transport in and around towns of workers is done with trucks. Taking an automobile ride, even in the back of an open truck, still seems a pleasure rather than a chore for these men and women, who will invariably—no matter if the sun broils or the rain pours—wave happily and unjealously at a foreigner passing them in his smug Western limousine.)

22

DAILY LIFE for older people in similar work to this girl's is different mainly because they'd be married. Consider a married man in his middle thirties, working in the Shanghai Tool Plant. He will be earning seventy yuan a month—he is skilled, and wages in Shanghai are somewhat higher than in Peking. He may be handling a new, Chinese-built lathe. These factories mix work and instruction; part of his time a colleague of his, just back from Rumania or Bulgaria, will teach him greater precision. If he is ambitious, he can eventually become an engineer while working, but this will not greatly increase his income. His wife used to work in the same factory, doing the same kind of work. With two children in school and a new baby, she quit and now has a part-time job in the nursery of the housing development where they live, earning twenty yuan a month.

The Kung Tjiang development where they have an apartment is four miles from the center of town. It was one of the earliest slum replacement projects after 1949 and does not compare very favorably with more recent ones. Nevertheless, there is a long waiting list for any of its eleven thousand units which may become free, and of late work has started to add two stories to some of the three-story buildings. Their apartment is screened from the landing by a door of bamboo matting only; behind it lies a little vestibule with two doors, one to the toilet, one to the kitchen. The toilet is the "pilgrim" type, just two foot rests and a hole in the floor. The kitchen has gas burners and a sink with running water. On each side of the kitchen is one room; to the left the bedroom where the parents sleep on a large low bed, covered with matting, and the baby in a wooden crib; to the right is the living room, with two cots for the school-age children.

The bedroom is bare but for the bed and the crib; the living room has a table with four chairs, and a dresser with a clock and a radio. On the wall are some family portraits, a picture of Mao, and a calendar with a pinup girl—not in a bathing suit, however, but in a sky-blue dress, framed by pink blossoming pear trees. All rooms are completely whitewashed and look more cheerful and less poor than this inventory would make them seem to be. The rent is a standard 5% of the family income, four yuan fifty in this case. Electricity and water are free; the cooking gas costs half a yuan a month. School fees for the children, both still in grade school, are twelve yuan a year for each; in high school they will be twenty-four yuan a year. The day nursery for a baby costs three yuan fifty a month, but since the mother of this family is home with the baby half the day and spends the other half as a worker in the nursery herself, she does not have to pay. Medical service is free for the father; for his family he pays 50% of the cost.

The factory runs trucks between the plant and the settlement for the transportation of some twenty employees who live there. There are also three bus lines into Shanghai. They have a sports field, a playground and a shopping center, a square block of buildings surrounded by a sidewalk under an arcading roof, with a department store, food store, barbershop and so on. Sixty thousand people live in the eleven thousand apartments; in summer and after school, the streets are teeming with children. The stores, like most Chinese stores, look well-kept.

The big settlement clinic is quite impressive. It has an X-ray machine as modern as the one on display at the Industries Fair in town, four dentist chairs, and twenty-two doctors. Some of these practice only the traditional Chinese medicine, acupuncture, and probably few or none of them would be up to Western university standards. But the pharmacy has many of the latest drugs, and although the place is packed at all hours by a flood of people, the nurses and doctors seem endlessly patient and even-tempered. Chinese medicine has only just emerged from the dark ages; there used to be a handful of modern hospitals run mainly by Westerners, plus the traditional doctors prescribing acupuncture and herbs for whoever could afford it. (Those doctors had to hang a lantern outside their houses for each patient who died, but many lanterns meant much experience and were thus not necessarily a deterrent.) "The people" kept themselves alive, or didn't, on their own, with the aid of a vast body of superstition and folklore, passed on from generation to generation. Twenty-five years ago, bread dipped in the fresh blood of executed criminals or Communists was still bought by them as a remedy for tuberculosis. They are far from used yet to the availability of all this medical aid, and they stream to these clinics as if it were a family outing.

The two older children of the lathe operator are in school seven hours a day, and they take turns in "community projects" such as raking leaves in the park, collecting melon rinds for fertilizer, or going out to plant tree saplings or mountain grass in a reforestation project in the hills. The husband's parents are both dead; the parents of the wife live in Chapu, a small town not far from Shanghai, on sixty yuan a month labor insurance. Grandfather is very old and weak; when he dies, his widow will move in with her daughter and son-in-law, who may then change to an apartment with one more little room. This man has now about as much free time and spending money as a European factory worker at the turn of the century. It depends on his personality what he does with them; vast amounts of free education are available to him, but he can obviously also take a chair out to the nearest grass field and smoke cigarets, and look at the sky. He will not escape the weekly evenings of politics; he may just sit through these, alienating no one, or decide to take an active part, become a representative of his section and start bustling about in committees and study groups. He probably does not own any books but may borrow from the library; he can take up sports, and take his wife bicycling on Sundays. Difference from the life of his European counterpart, there is a total absence of pubs or bars in his life. Once in a great while he may get drunk with some friends in someone's house, but he'll walk home quietly just the same. If he created a disturbance —a very rare phenomenon indeed—his name would be mentioned with disapprobation at the next meeting of the tenants' committee, to the great embarrassment of himself and his family.

23

DAILY LIFE for a couple on a higher level of income and education: a man working in the national travel agency in Canton, married to a girl who just graduated as a physician. He earns seventy-five yuan a month, and so does she. Out of this combined income of a hundred and fifty yuan, they pay only one yuan ninety a month rent for a one-room apartment with a kitchenette in a building owned by the travel agency, a nice if somewhat decrepit old house on what was once the foreign concession in Canton, Shameen. They eat breakfast together at eight (tea and wheat cakes, or rice porridge), after which he walks to his office and she takes the bus to the hospital. They both have their lunches and dinners at work, for which they pay ten to twelve yuan a month; they meet again around seven in the evening. Sunday is free for both of them, and on that day they go shopping and cook their own dinner and supper.

They save quite a lot of money, and the wife recently bought herself a piano, which cost 850 yuan, out of her savings. *Lao dung* they do within their own ken; she sometimes puts in a week of nurse duty at the hospital—which would seem a waste in a country so short of doctors, but which again must serve the purpose of "eliminating contempt for manual work," and he has occasionally volunteered for work as porter or waiter in a hotel. He once did a month's work in the country—"Good for your health," he said. He never does physical exercises though; he prefers "to sit in the park with a book." My Peking doctor attended a political session for the hospital staff every Saturday afternoon from two to five: Canton is more lax in these matters and the girl's hospital has no such rule. In fact, neither she nor her husband talks or seems to think much about politics. But they are both children of very poor peasants; and their loyalty and respect for their government seem way beyond any doubt or discussion.

These two people have been married for three years. By choice, they have no children, and they are obviously living on such a relatively high level because of that; they are determined to keep it that way at least for the time being. Such a decision is no problem; in this case obviously not, since the girl is a doctor, but it wouldn't be for any other woman either. Birth control is again acknowledged state policy. There are courses and clinics for the purpose and contraceptives are very cheap; the Chinese are also working on a locally made birth control pill. The officially given reasoning behind it is not fear of overpopulation or lagging food production, but feminine emancipation: "Woman cannot be a true equal of man if her body is exhausted by frequent childbearing, and her career cut short by too many household duties."

The Cantonese couple are within their own world very much "with it," working hard enough, but more self-indulgent perhaps and more elegant than most of those around them; life in Canton, with its many outdoor cafés and theaters, beautiful river sidewalks and generally lighter mood, can be made quite pleasant. The girl is interested in clothes, too, and manages to make them both look more or less well-turned-out; their apartment is attractive.

It must indeed be the native decorative sense of China which has saved its cities from the drabness which the leveling processes of socialism or communism produced in Eastern Europe. No reasons of state have suppressed this talent. For instance: the cheapest notepad of Chinese stationery has a little design in color—some bamboos with a bird, a country house, a mountain scene—in the corner of each page, and *each* page has a *different* design. Chinese stamps are a delight. In various arts and crafts factories, old men train young men and girls in jade and ivory cutting, pottery and painting; and here—as if there were no such things as Five-Year Plans and Great Leaps—one artist spends an entire month painting a picture on the inside of a little glass flask, using a tiny brush with a ninety-degree bend in it. These articles sell for little money, for no effort is made to recover what it costs to produce them. The Canton couple have some of these things in their room, including a print in the classical tradition on the wall. (Women in art workshops is an innovation; traditionally, no woman was allowed to touch ivory.)

The young man usually goes to work without a jacket and tie and wearing espadrilles; some days he wears a regular suit. No matter how hot it may be, however, he wouldn't dream of appearing on the street in a T-shirt or shorts. In Imperial China, the intellectuals wore long gowns, the workmen short ones; and in a present-day summer crowd it seems as if the same line were still drawn, but now between the long trousers of professional men and white-collar workers, and the shorts of those who do manual labor. The young man will, on hot days, also carry a black hand fan, which isn't in the least considered effeminate.

I paid a visit to an industry canteen in the company of this travel agency man; we were asked again and again if we really liked their food, and we kept saying that it was very good. But when we were outside and I said that I thought it had really been good (which was true), he would not believe me.

I: "I'm not trying to be polite."

He (after a silence): "Well—I prefer another style of cooking."

I: "I liked it as much as the food in my hotel."

At which he laughed unbelievingly.

24

CANTON in the Pearl River delta, or Guangjoe as its inhabitants stubbornly go on calling it, was the first Chinese town seen by Western seamen. The Portuguese showed up here in the early fifteen hundreds with two ships and established a trend by stealing and buying from, and selling and talking about Christianity to, every Chinese in sight. Canton had seen foreign traders before: once many thousand Persian, Moslem and Jewish merchants lived in the town. But they had long since gone (those that weren't killed in one war or another), only leaving behind one of the oldest mosques in China; and they had been a very different species from the fidgety Westerners. In an effort to keep the Portuguese at a distance, China gave them the tip of Macao peninsula, at the western shore of the river mouth, for their purposes. It did not work out, of course, and soon foreigners were back in town; eventually they took the eastern end too (Hong Kong), and they went on from there until they were right in the Forbidden City of Peking. Now we, the West, are more or less back where we started from in China, at the two tips of the Pearl River mouth; and the eastern one, the British Crown Colony, has all but finished off its competitor, Macao. Macao, Portuguese since 1557, has through the years remained the one piece of territory the Chinese ceded more or less voluntarily; and during World War II it was the only spot (six square miles) in all of Southeast Asia not controlled by Japan.

It is a decrepit and rather dreary little town now, but it is a kind of colonial reserve where one can still watch some of the old China.

Narrow beggary streets are filled with outdoor shops, and coolies, with an occasional Mercedes squeezing its way through; half a dozen junks, probably smugglers, are anchored in the silted-up harbor; at the quay where the boat from Hong Kong docks, taxi and pedicab drivers outshout each other for the few passengers coming ashore. The main street lies abandoned in the violent sunshine; in one dark, heavily air-conditioned café the local notables sit around, drinking rum and nursing old-fashioned *cafards,* looking like actors in a Jean Gabin movie of the thirties. They wear sloppy, wrinkled white suits, and in their tanned faces the features of China and Portugal seem to mingle; their eyes are tired but they have in their gestures and words that infinite relaxedness of men who at all times in their lives have been able to satisfy immediately any hunger, any thirst, any lust they have felt.

Behind garden walls and palms lie the old European mansions, filled with decayed Mediterranean furniture, in which men eke out their forgotten glories; one bright new building houses the casino and here a throng of undefinable visitors from who knows where sit around losing their money. Every evening as it darkens, a very prim-looking gentleman with a white moustache sits down for an early dinner at his own reserved table in the empty dining room of the only first-class hotel, and slowly takes his napkin out of a silver ring with his initials. At the taxi stand across from the post office, two German businessmen from Hong Kong vainly try to explain in loud voices to a cabdriver that they want to visit a brothel; in Macao these are discreetly and well hidden. Portuguese noncoms on patrol go by on bicycles, with sten guns across their backs; they ignore all traffic rules and stare at every Chinese until he looks away; they are a different race and species from the old men in the cafés and look like killers in a comic strip. The last ferry of the day returns the tourists to Hong Kong; and Macao is left in its abandoned sleep.

Canton now is as bustling a place as in the descriptions given by its visitors of the early nineteenth century when 30,000 chests of opium, each weighing 133 lbs., were yearly imported here by England, France and the United States; and Western merchants arrive again, though by train from Hong Kong with visas from the Chinese consul rather than by sailing up the Pearl. Canton stages an industries export fair in spring and autumn, and on those occasions Europeans in numbers not seen here in a long time flood the town, which must at least partly account for Canton's sophistication toward foreigners. There is also, of course, its nearness to Hong Kong, its role as the great port of Chinese emigration, and perhaps most important of all, the southern and rebellious traits of the Cantonese themselves.

The Cantonese have played their part in this revolution and in most of the revolutions before; by the same token they now seem somewhat less impressed by the wisdoms of Peking than their more northern compatriots, and of a particularly carefree cast of mind. Hung Hsin-chuan, of the Taiping Heavenly Kingdom rebellion, was a Cantonese, and so was Sun Yat-sen who set up government here in 1917. (Chiang Kai-shek joined him in Canton in 1922.) On the 23rd of June, 1925, a British man-of-war in the harbor opened fire on student demonstrators of the "May 30 Movement" and killed two hundred. Two years later, Canton had a brief spell as a town ruled by a Communist commune based on the model of Paris of 1871. In 1938 the Japanese occupied it, after the Pearl River Bridge had been blown up in vain to stop them. In 1949 the Communists took the town, after the Kuomintang had again in vain blown up the rebuilt bridge. Now the bridge has been rebuilt for the third time, and the towering Ai Chun Hotel near it, which had been painted a drab brown during the war to make it less conspicuous to raiding planes, has been painted white once more. Ai Chun means "Love for the Masses," but the hotel already had that name in its prewar capitalist days. Hong Kong rumor had it that Canton, preparing for one more episode of war, had antiaircraft guns on its roofs and was evacuating women and children, but as of December, 1965, no trace of such activities was discernible to a visitor.

Canton has many parks with outdoor amusements in Chinese fashion; these are free now but without the tedium usually associated with gratis public entertainment. There is an open-air opera house in one park, and near it an open-air theater. There is an outdoor aquarium and various sideshows, including a theater with life-size puppets in beautiful old costumes operated from a platform above the stage. And all this is set in subtropical flora under a southern sky in which the Milky Way (which in Chinese is called "The Silver River") stands out even when looked at from the middle of town; and it is packed with a crowd, much more lively than the men and women of Peking (not to mention Shanghai), talking away in the southern language which has eight different voice pitches and which the northerners, who cannot understand a word of it, call *niao yu* which means birds' chatter.

Canton is a water town, dominated by the Pearl River, the Chu Kiang; its boat people, living on more than fifty thousand houseboats, used to be famous. They were a tribe apart, who had no schools, who were allowed to marry only among themselves, and who by law had to go barefoot when they came into town. Now there are only ten thousand boats left; the boat people are housed in new apartment blocks put up on the south shore of the river. Presently they will all be ashore. The young ones are happy, obviously better off; the old ones, used to the freedom and the dirt of their boats, their out-of-bounds society in every sense of the word, seem lost in their new little flats with narrow staircases, doorbells, and garbage collections. (Traveling from north to south, Soochow in Kiangsu Province is the first water town in this Cantonese style, with people living on the river, tile-roofed houses in almost Mediterranean patterns, and humpbacked bridges as in Venice.)

Canton is not a classless town or a proletarian one; its character is much more diverse than that. Like other Chinese cities, it still has its very poor, but, living in a blessed climate, they seem less miserable here. It has its laborers, dressed if they belong to the older generation, as if it were their uniform, in the peculiar black waxed cloth of the Chinese south, indestructible but also incomprehensibly hot (Sicilian peasant women wear a similar baffling black under their *solleone,* the lion-sun). Then Canton has thousands of students attending Sun Yat-sen University which lies in a park behind a large pond, at the river; a wooden jetty from which a few old men fish, moors the squat river boats on which they travel to their classes. Canton has its very mild equivalent of the jet set; it includes a number of students who sit around in the outdoor cafés and the six classic restaurants of the town. Finally, Canton has a unique group of leisurely rich: overseas Chinese who have returned to their motherland for a vacation or, more often, to end here their days on earth. They live in a hybrid world of communism trimmed with bourgeois indulgences bought with hard currency, in houses especially built for them with air-conditioning, refrigerators, and all the other comforts decidedly not of home but of abroad.

Canton's Bund runs East-West, and the sun rises and sets right over the river. Three waterways merge just about in its middle at the White Goose Pool, where under the Ming dynasty a peasant rebel, trapped by soldiers coming from all directions, was carried off by a white goose. Shameen, which used to be the British-French concession——made into an island by canals surrounding it from the river back into the river ——looks out onto the White Goose Pool. It lies quiet and green under the dense trees; children run around and play tag in the middle of its streets, among them oddly a white boy or girl here and there, offspring of some European diplomat.

Shameen's stone East Bridge and West Bridge were once guarded by Gurkas, and some of the cannon are still there which kept the natives away. Fifty who were killed on one occasion have their memorial here now, with the usual inscription and the usual wilted wreath. ("Zest rather than danger is added to residence in Shameen by reason of the occasional disturbances in Canton," Carl Crow wrote in his guidebook of 1921.) In those days, sedan chairs with four bearers each used to wait under the trees of Shameen for foreigners going into Canton, many of whose streets were too narrow for rickshaws.

On a sudden cool evening, as may come upon Canton late in the year, the fog from the river and the canals creeps up over Shameen and fills the streets with a grey diffused light in which the street lamps make soft rings. It is easy then to imagine afoot under those dripping trees the ghosts of all the men who had a go at China in their days—the pirates, Jesuits, teachers, traders, thieves and opium merchants, the generals, the pimps, the missionaries and the con men.

"But in the mist, through which a heron winds its way, their footsteps are lost forever—"

25

THE OTHER WORLD AWAITS at the Shumchun border station on the Canton-Kowloon line. "It must have been awful," a New Yorker said to me when I told him I had been in China, and when I answered, "No, coming out was awful," he gave me an uncertain look, not sure whether I was joking or had been brainwashed by the Communists. But it was awful. After a visit of any length to Eastern Europe—no matter how much understanding one may have for the former backwardness of these countries, the destruction wrought upon them by Germany and the enormous efforts made—there is a sense of relief in returning to the Western world, to the lights, the liberty, the cafés, the magazines, the women, the cars, of Paris or Amsterdam. No such feeling accompanies the transition across the frontier between China and the British Empire at

Shumchun. There is a change of trains there; a Free World porter carries the luggage to the British train (and demands more money than the fare was from Canton to the border); signs appear, "Beware of pickpockets"; beggars put their hands through the windows; the carriages are filthy and there is an indignant scramble for seats; an endless stream of peddlers make their appearance and march through the train, all offering bottles of Coca-Cola as if this were the one symbol of the Western world, the thing we must all have been pining for under communism. The train goes as far as Kowloon only; taxicabs are not allowed on the ferry to Hong Kong, and thus the traveler celebrates his re-entry into his own world by marching through concrete dockyard corridors while a sweating coolie runs after him, bent double under his suitcases; there will be a wicked argument about the tip once the ferry has docked; a fight for a cab; and then Hong Kong in its artificiality, its ads against bad breath, bad figures, bad skin, and in favor of beauty, popularity, and getting rich; with its tired American widows hunting for bargains, and its sad sailors being gypped out of the sin they had been told to expect.

Hong Kong is not Chinese (and those who report on China from Hong Kong are at as much of a disadvantage as they would be writing about the United States from the vantage point of a San Juan resort hotel); it is the West, and not at its best, in spite of its modernity. It has assuredly more freedom and more food than China, but it also has the cheapest of values; it is jungle and chaos. It made China, with all the many bounds put on the inhabitants there, seem orderly and moral, and in spite of China's poverty, it made it seem glamorous. "Glamorous" is a very strange adjective to come to mind for

China, I realize that; but standing at the window of my beautifully comfortable room in the Hong Kong Hilton, and looking down upon the equally beautiful and celebrated view, I thought that China had been glamorous.

The landscape as seen from the train had not changed much as we left China and rode through the British Crown Colony; the only visible difference was the many cars appearing on the roads. They came as a shock. For a long time a new Hillman of a shiny grey kept up with us; a pretty young woman was driving it (she was blonde, too) with two children in the back seat; then she turned into a sideroad and stopped in the parking lot of an office of the Shell Oil Company. Evidently, I thought, she came to pick up her equally young and handsome husband—not a Western Imperialist he, just a nice guy and a promising junior executive. It was a perfectly set scene from an Anglo-Saxon *Dolce Vita,* our way of life, what we want and what we can get if we work for it.

It filled me with a vague nostalgia that I could not explain to myself—nostalgia perhaps for those happy days when our Western world seemed so good and wise, and it seemed so proper and natural that our own blond children should inherit the earth.

Contrasting sights on the new China scene, which include a Chinese-built freighter (the *Hong Qi* or *Red Flag*); the